T5-CQC-083

COLUMBUS

A Smart, Sustainable City

COLUMBUS

A Smart, Sustainable City

Broos Campbell and Tina G. Rubin

Acknowledgements

Columbus: A Smart, Sustainable City was produced in cooperation with the City of Columbus. Cherbo Publishing Group gratefully acknowledges its important contribution to this publication.

 cherbo publishing group, inc.

Cherbo Publishing Group, Inc.
Encino, California 91316
© 2012 by Cherbo Publishing Group, Inc.
All rights reserved. Published 2012.

Printed in Canada
By Friesens

ISBN: 978-1-882933-91-4

Library of Congress Cataloging-in-Publication data
Campbell, B. D.
A pictorial guide highlighting Columbus' economic and social advantages.
2011941571

Visit the CPG Web site at
www.cherbopub.com.

president	JACK C. CHERBO
chief operating officer	ELAINE HOFFMAN
editorial director	LINDA CHASE
creative director	PERI A. HOLGUIN
senior designer	THEODORE E. YEAGER.
sales administrator	JOAN K. BAKER
senior project coordinator	PATRICIA DE LEONARD
client services coordinator	LESLIE E. SHAW
administrative assistant	BILL WAY
eastern regional manager	MARCIA WEISS
publisher's representative	MARY HANLEY

The information in this publication is the most recent available and has been carefully researched to ensure accuracy. Cherbo Publishing Group, Inc. cannot and does not guarantee either the correctness of all information furnished it or the complete absence of errors, including omissions.

To purchase additional copies of this book, contact Joan Baker at Cherbo Publishing Group: jbaker@cherbopub.com or phone 818.783.0040 ext. 27.

Above: The new Main Street Bridge, which opened in 2010, connects downtown Columbus with Franklinton. The first inclined single-rib tied arch bridge in the United States, this unique structure features a three-lane deck for vehicle traffic and a walkway for pedestrians and cyclists.

CONTENTS

PROFILES IN EXCELLENCE

The following corporations and organizations, which are profiled in this publication, have displayed excellence in their fields and made a valuable contribution to the growth and success of the Columbus area.

BUSINESS VISIONARIES

The following companies and organizations are recognized as innovators in their fields and have played a prominent role in this publication, as they have in the Columbus area.

Cardinal Health
7000 Cardinal Place
Dublin, OH 43017

The Ohio State University Medical Center
410 West 10th Avenue
Columbus, Ohio 43210
Phone: 614.293.5123
Email: osucareconnection@osumc.edu
Web site: medicalcenter.osu.edu

Quick Solutions, Inc.
440 Polaris Parkway, Suite 500
Westerville, OH 43082
Phone: 614.825.8000
Fax: 614.825.8006
Website: www.quicksolutions.com
Facebook: facebook.com/quicksolutions
Twitter: @quick_solutions
Leading IT Consulting Firm

Nationwide
1 Nationwide Plaza
Columbus, OH 43215
Phone: 800.882.2822
Web site: www.nationwide.com
www.facebook.com/nationwide
www.twitter.com/nationwide

Worthington Industries, Inc.
200 Old Wilson Bridge Road
Columbus, OH 43085
Phone: 614.438.3210
Fax: 614.438.7948
Web site: www.worthingtonindustries.com

FOREWORD

Welcome to the City of Columbus.

Dear Friends:

2012 marks the bicentennial of the City of Columbus. There is so much to be proud of as the city reflects on its 200-year history. This book celebrates Columbus' accomplishments of the past and opportunities for the future.

Throughout the book, you will see an emphasis on the efforts being made throughout the community to become increasingly environmentally sustainable. This effort, branded as Get Green Columbus, has many benefits for our individual and collective wellbeing as we strive to fulfill our mission to be the best city in the nation in which to live, work, and raise a family.

To fully understand what makes Columbus so special, I invite you to come and experience the city for yourself. I am confident that you will enjoy what you discover here as you interact with our residents, businesses, and organizations.

Sincerely,

Michael B. Coleman
Mayor

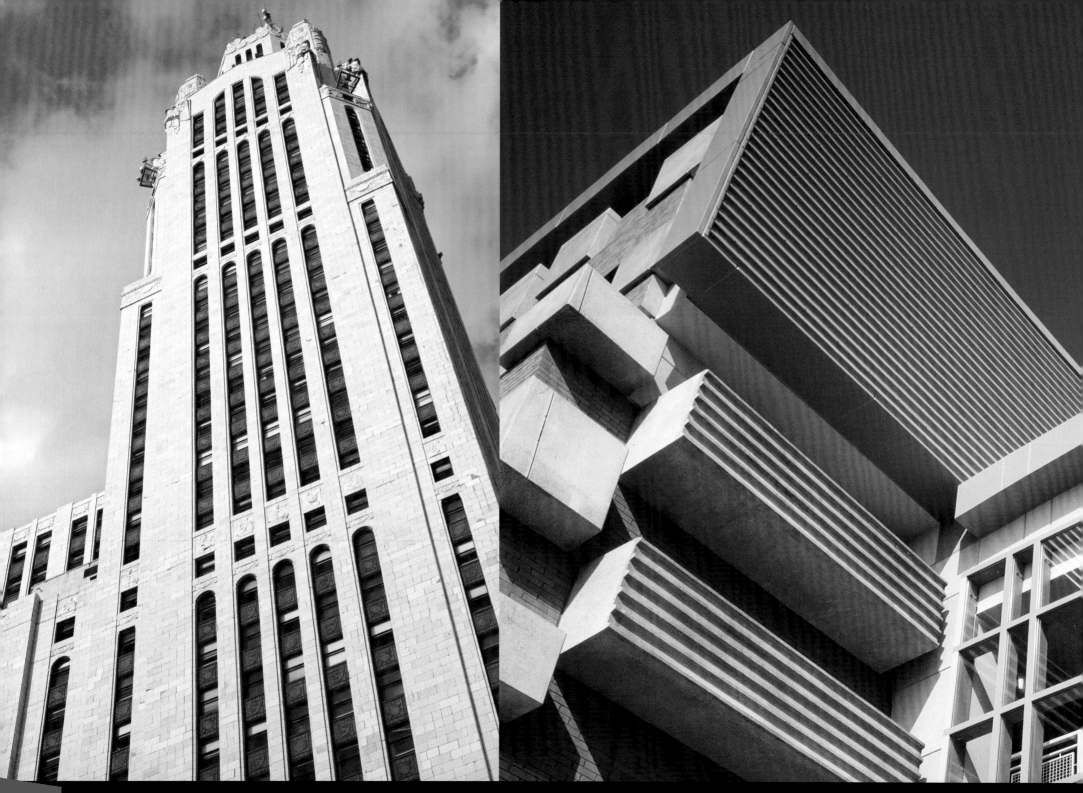

This spread, from left: Brutus Buckeye, the Ohio State University mascot, revs up the crowd; the Blue Jackets skate against an NHL opponent at Nationwide Arena; the Columbus Crew faces the Philadelphia Union in an MLS Eastern Conference match at Crew Stadium.

THE "GREENING" OF COLUMBUS

1800s–1900s

Columbus Savings & Trust Company, ca. 1900-1915.

1910
Columbus Department of Recreation and Parks is formed, which now holds public open spaces, nature preserves, including forests and restored streams, and wetlands.

1967
City's first trail is built along the banks of the Olentangy River.

1968
The Ohio State University (OSU) creates the School of Natural Resources (now the School of Environment and Natural Resources), offering a master's degree and undergraduate courses in subjects ranging from conservation to fisheries management.

1972
COTA is established with voters approving $800,000 transit levy.

Ohio EPA is established to ensure compliance with federal acts regarding air quality, drinking water, surface water, solid and hazardous waste management, and emergency and remedial response to contamination.

1989
Faculty from the colleges of agriculture, biological sciences, and engineering propose an interdisciplinary Environmental Science Graduate Program, an expansion of the existing Environmental Biology Graduate Program at OSU.

1863
Columbus streetcars begin operating. Fares are a nickel—and remain a nickel till the system is disbanded after World War II.

1908
Scioto Water Purification Plant and Pumping Station on Dublin Road combines purification with water softening.

1969
The Cuyahoga River in northeastern Ohio catches on fire, resulting in pollution control measures that include the Clean Water Act and the Great Lakes Water Quality Agreement.

1970
President Nixon creates the U.S. Environmental Protection Agency by executive order. Ohio is part of the agency's Region 5, which also includes Minnesota, Wisconsin, Michigan, Illinois, and Indiana.

1984
The Big Darby, located on the west side of Columbus is designated a state Scenic River. The Big and Little Darby are later both named National Scenic Rivers in 1994.

1987
The O'Shaughnessy Dam begins operating five-megawatt turbines to generate hydroelectricity.

1999
Clean Fuels Ohio is founded as part of the Columbus Health Department. It becomes an independent nonprofit in 2002.

The New Millennium

Thompson Library at The Ohio State University.

Mayor Coleman creates Office of Environmental Stewardship and brings together a group of advisors known as the Mayor's Green Team.

Mayor Coleman's Executive Order 2005-02 outlines city fleet vehicle idling and fuel conservation conduct, including an anti-idling policy.

2006
Ten local jurisdictions, including the City of Columbus, officially form the Big Darby Accord to protect sensitive and naturally acclaimed ecosystem.

City receives MORPC Clean Air Award.

Mayor Coleman creates Central Ohio Green Pact; 12other central Ohio jurisdictions sign pact.

City releases Bicentennial Bikeways Plan to encourage residents to shift from single-occupancy vehicles to biking, walking, and public transportation.

2008
City's Division of Fleet Management issues first Green Fleet Action, conserving fuel and finding innovative methods to incorporate alternative fuels, including Compressed Natural Gas (CNG), flex fuels, hybrids, and all-electric vehicles.

2000
Mayor Michael B. Coleman takes office.

2004
The Ohio 4-H Center and the Thompson Library renovation at OSU receive LEED certification.

2005
Mayor Coleman's "Memo" outlines a path toward responsible, sustainable growth that includes addressing air quality and landfill issues, improving recycling efforts, promoting green businesses, constructing green buildings, and establishing an alternative green building code.

2007
Columbus holds first citywide Earth Day celebration after a hiatus of more than 10 years. The event grows to become the largest celebration and volunteer worksite in the world.

Mayor Coleman signs U.S. Mayors Climate Protection Agreement. Mayor Coleman issues Executive Order 2007-02, which requires city departments to conserve paper and purchase paper with a minimum of 30% post consumer recycled content.

A compressed natural-gas sticker on a Honda natural-gas vehicle (NGV).

THE "GREENING" OF COLUMBUS

The New Millennium

A class field trip at Olentangy River Westland Research Park.

Two low-head dams impeding water quality on Alum Creek are removed with help from the City in an effort spearheaded by the Friend of Alum Creek and Tributaries.

2009
The American Recovery and Reinvestment Act (ARRA) provides the City with funding to update inefficient city equipment, create bike transportation amenities, and build rain gardens at Hoover, Griggs and O'Shaughnessy reservoirs.

First LEED Platinum-certified single-family home in Ohio becomes available for viewing on North 21st Street in Columbus.

Government Fleet Magazine recognizes Columbus' municipal fleet as 22nd Greenest Fleet greenest in the nation. City receives Clean Fuels Ohio Champion Award.

Columbus unveils its Ohio Bicentennial Bikeways Master Plan.

City issues Air Quality Alert Action plan outlining steps to minimize pollution and protect health of its employees on days when pollution levels reach unhealthy levels.

Mayor Coleman launches GreenSpot program to guide green-minded residents and businesses in their efforts to become more environmentally friendly. www.GreenSpotColumbus.org

Sustainability advocacy group SustainLane ranks Columbus as most improved among the nation's 50 largest cities, up from last in 2006, for its environmental knowledge, green economy, and master bike plan.

OSU Olentangy River Wetland Research Park is formally designated as the United States' 24th Ramsar Wetland of International Importance.

Buckeye Bullet 2, the world's first research race car to be powered by hydrogen fuel cells, averages a record-breaking 302.9 mph at Bonneville Salt Flats. An updated version, the Venturi Buckeye Bullet 2.5, reaches a peak speed of 320 mph in 2010.

City is designated a Bicycle Friendly Community by the League of American Bicyclists.

City wins American Council of Engineering's Award of Excellence for Bike User Map, a collaborative project with MORPC. Columbus named *Bicycling Magazine*'s New Best City for Cycling.

Mayor Coleman introduces 10-Year Reform and Efficiency Action Plan, recommending continuation and expansion of weatherization, efficient lighting, HVAC system upgrades, and other efficiency measures.

2010
Mayor Coleman issues Green Memo II, the second five-year plan for sustainability for the City of Columbus.

New Main Street Bridge, the first single-rib tied arch bridge in the country, opens to motor vehicles, with separate bicycle, and pedestrian accommodations.

City wins MORPC Energy & Air Award, GreenSpot Program wins SWACO Emerald Award in Education category; Mayor Coleman wins SWACO Emerald Award for Leadership.

Whetstone Park of Roses is named America's Best Rose Garden.

2011
City breaks ground on first compressed natural gas fueling station.

Mayor Coleman receives the Green Energy Ohio Public Official of the Year Award.

Columbus is U.S. Chamber/ Siemens Sustainable Community Award Finalist.

Columbus receives SWACO Emerald Award, Education category for GreenSpot Program; Mayor Coleman receives Leadership Award.

Scioto Mile Park, with downtown Columbus in the background.

SEEKING A SUSTAINABLE FUTURE

PART ONE

This page: A dazzling fountain display lights up the night at Bicentennial Park on the Scioto Mile in downtown Columbus. Opposite page: This replica of the *Santa Maria*, one of Christopher Columbus' sailing ships, is moored on the Scioto River.

Quality of Life

REDISCOVERING COLUMBUS

If Christopher Columbus were to revisit the New World today, he would surely seek out the thriving metropolis that bears his name. Celebrating its bicentennial in 2012, the City of Columbus has navigated 200 years of proud history and is charting a course for a limitless future.

Columbus is worthy of rediscovery. It is the 15th-largest city in the United States and the state capital of Ohio. It produced golfing great Jack Nicklaus, artist George Bellows, and cartoonist/humorist James Thurber. It is home to the nation's oldest commercial peanut butter manufacturer and the only maker of metal whistles in the United States. And it is home to The Ohio State Buckeyes.

Under the leadership of Mayor Michael B. Coleman, who took office in 1999, Columbus has emerged in the past decade as a leader in green initiatives, redevelopment, and quality of life. Ohio's largest city, with a population of 787,000, Columbus is located in Franklin County, which has a population of more than one million. The eight-county metropolitan area (Franklin, Delaware, Fairfield, Licking, Madison, Morrow, Union, and Pickaway) has a combined population of 1.7 million. Columbus lies within a one-day drive or a one-hour flight of 60 percent of the population of the United States and Canada. An attractive location for business, it is headquarters for 14 of the top 1,000 companies in the United States, including Abercrombie & Fitch, American Electric Power, Big Lots, and Nationwide Insurance.

CHAPTERONE

Education is a cornerstone of life in central Ohio, where 115,000 college students attend 26 colleges and universities. Columbus is one of the few cities in the country where recent college graduates have chosen to live as young professionals rather than move somewhere else, according to The Brookings Institute. This concentration of brainpower has helped place Columbus at no. 1 on Forbes' list of Top Ten Up-and-Coming Tech Cities.

Canvassing the City

Columbus offers a vibrant mix of history, culture, and commerce. The downtown Arena District, a 95-acre planned development, features restaurants, nightclubs, and entertainment venues, including the Arena Grand Theatre, an upscale movie theater, and the LC, an indoor/outdoor music hall styled after the House of Blues. Marked by 17 lighted arches spanning High Street, the Short North Arts District features the city's largest collection of art galleries, with eclectic works by local, national, and international artists. On the first Saturday

of each month, most businesses stay open late for the popular Gallery Hop. The district also has a variety of restaurants, pubs, and specialty shops. One block west is historic North Market, which purveys fresh and prepared foods, flowers, ethnic cuisine, and unique gifts.

German Village, a 233-acre restored neighborhood just south of downtown, was originally settled in the mid-1800s by German immigrants and is listed on the National Register of Historic Places. Along its tree-lined, brick-paved streets are lovingly restored redbrick homes, wrought-iron fences, beautiful gardens, and enticing restaurants and specialty retailers. West of German Village, the Brewery District, traditionally known as the Old German Brewing District, has been revitalized, providing unique shopping and entertainment venues.

The historic Franklinton area, where Columbus had its roots, is being transformed into a vibrant urban center for the artistic and creative community through a partnership between the city, Urban Smart Growth, and the Franklinton community. The revitalized neighborhood will feature performance and event venues, music, art galleries, and restaurants.

The King Arts Complex, located in one of the city's oldest African-American neighborhoods on the Near East side, celebrates the contributions of African Americans throughout history with dynamic art exhibitions, concerts, and theater and dance performances. Designed to resemble a slave ship, the permanent interactive exhibit, "Cargo: The Middle Passage," provides a visceral experience of the long, arduous journey from Africa to the New World.

Art of the Matter

During her tour of the United States in 1934, Gertrude Stein discovered that unlike Oakland, where "there is no there there," Columbus was worthy of notice by the art world. "In the Columbus Museum of Art I came into a room and it was a pleasant one," she wrote in *Everybody's Autobiography*. "It was all Cubist and good Picassos and Juan Gris and others but really good ones. There had never been anything like that either in choice or quality or like that in any other museum."

Stein would find much to admire in the museum's current collection of 19th- and early 20th-century works, photographs, and folk art. Herself an avant-garde figure, she would appreciate the collection of American Social Commentary Art, 1930–1970, described as "unquestionably the most important collection of its kind in the country" by Virginia Mecklenburg, Chief Curator of Smithsonian American Art Museum. Following a $6.9 million renovation, the museum's 1931 Italian Renaissance revival building on Broad Street reopened in January 2011.

Upgrades were made throughout the museum, with the first floor reconfigured as a Center for Creativity.

Being a center of education, Columbus combines instruction with interactive fun for the entire family. A National Historic Landmark and a masterpiece of 19th-century Greek Revival architecture, the Ohio Statehouse was completed in 1861 and restored in 1996. At the interactive Ohio Statehouse Museum, visitors can delve into Ohio history and brush up on their rhetoric by giving a State of the State address. Headquarters of the Ohio Historical Society, the Ohio Historical Center houses a museum showcasing Ohio's history from the Ice Age to 1970. Described by the 1989 *Smithsonian Guide to Historic America* as "probably the finest museum in America devoted to pre-European history," the museum also hosts temporary exhibits throughout the year.

Ranked the number one science center in the country for families by *Parents Magazine*, COSI features more than 300 interactive exhibits throughout its exhibition areas, including the outdoor Big Science Park. COSI also hosts world-class traveling exhibitions throughout the year.

This page: The newly renovated Columbus Museum of Art features spacious, well-lit galleries. Opposite page, from left: Brewers Gate, an urban development in Columbus, won an AIA Merit Award in 2008; the Arena District is Columbus' downtown entertainment district.

15

This page: Dancers perform at Festival Latino in downtown Columbus. Opposite page, from left: Columbus' historic Southern Theatre opened in 1896 and was beautifully restored prior to its reopening in 1998; the coral reef at the Columbus Zoo mesmerizes a visitor.

The performing arts in Columbus are equally robust. The Columbus Association for the Performing Arts (CAPA) is one of America's premier presenters of national and international performing artists and classic films, with venues in Columbus and New Haven, Connecticut, and presenting partnerships throughout Ohio. The Contemporary American Theatre Company (CATCO), Central Ohio's only professional resident theater company, has an extensive repertoire that includes classic, contemporary, and new works.

Downtown Columbus' historic theaters are home to the Columbus Symphony, BalletMet, Broadway Across America-Columbus, Columbus Jazz Orchestra, ProMusica Chamber Orchestra, Opera Columbus, and many other performing arts groups.

Columbus' popular annual events include Columbus Arts Festival, Jazz & RibFest, Red, White & Boom!, First Night Columbus, and the Ohio State Fair,

which is worth attending just to have a Schmidt's sausage. The city hosts numerous ethnic festivals, including Oktoberfest, Festival Latino, the Asian Festival, the Greek Festival, and the Italian Festival.

Columbus Au Naturel

Flora and fauna have found a hospitable environment in Columbus. Voted the favorite zoo in America by *USA Travel Guide*, the Columbus Zoo and Aquarium is a picturesque setting of naturalistic wildlife habitats for 8,800 animals representing 650 species from around the globe. Recognized for its success in breeding cheetahs and lowland gorillas, the zoo provides more than $1 million annually to support more than 70 conservation projects worldwide.

Just east of downtown, the Franklin Park Conservatory and Botanical Garden's 73,000 square feet of greenhouse feature horticulture from a wide variety of climate zones, including the signature 1895 Victorian glass Palm House housing more than 40 species of palms., A signature collection from the internationally acclaimed glass artist Dale Chihuly and a permanent light installation by world-renowned artist James Turrell are also found here. The American Community Garden Association makes its home among the live-fire cooking theater and the herb and vegetable gardens at the Conservatory's Scotts Miracle-Gro Community Garden Campus. Georges Seurat's famous postimpressionist land-scape, *A Sunday Afternoon on the Island of La Grande Jatte*, is re-created in a whimsical topiary display at Old Deaf School Park in downtown Columbus.

Columbus has added to its existing greenspace with the Scioto Mile, a new one-mile stretch of parkland stretching from the Arena District on the north end of downtown Columbus to Whittier Peninsula on the south. A grand esplanade and green corridor, The Promenade on the Scioto Mile parallels Civic Center Drive from Broad Street to Rich Street. The promenade connects Battelle Riverfront Park with the John W. Galbreath Bicentennial Park, which features a 15,000-square-foot water fountain, cafe, and bandshell.

Through a unique partnership between the City of Columbus, Metro Parks, and Audubon Ohio, the Whittier Peninsula is being transformed into a thriving ecosystem for birds and wetland foliage. The Scioto Audubon Metro Park, a 94-acre oasis on the peninsula near downtown Columbus, is used as a stopover by thousands of birds migrating from Central and South America. Hayden Falls Park, located on the west side of the Scioto River, is a unique gorge habitat that

only occurs along the western shore. Home to a 35-foot waterfall, this ecosystem shelters rare and endangered plants. At Big Darby Creek, a State and National Scenic River, trails for walking and biking line much of the Big Darby greenway as well as the other main waterways in Columbus, including the Olentangy River, Scioto River, Alum Creek, and Big Walnut Creek.

Sports Report

From the opening kick-off of the college football season to the crack of the bat on opening day, Columbus is among the nation's great sports cities. The Columbus Clippers, the Triple-A affiliate of the Cleveland Indians, play home games at Huntington Park, a 10,000 seat, state-of-the art-stadium that opened in April 2009 and was named the no. 1 new ballpark by *Ballpark Digest* and Ballparks.com. In its 20th anniversary issue, *Baseball America* recognized the Clippers as the top minor league franchise.

The Ohio State University arenas offer exciting sports action. Ohio Stadium is one of the largest in college football, with 102,329 seats. The home field for The Ohio State Buckeyes, the stadium underwent a $194 million renovation that was completed in 2001. Affectionately known as the Horseshoe for its shape, it has been the site of epic battles with the archrival Michigan Wolverines. The Schottenstein Center, a 20,000-seat multi-purpose arena that opened in 1998, hosts the men's and women's basketball teams, the men's ice hockey team, and a variety of other sporting events, concerts, and shows.

Nationwide Arena, which was ranked in 2004 as the no. 1 stadium experience in professional sports by *ESPN The Magazine*, is home ice for the Columbus Blue Jackets, Ohio's only National Hockey League team. The Columbus Crew, the 2008 MLS Cup Champions, play in the 22,500-seat Columbus Crew Stadium, the first soccer-specific MLS stadium in the United States.

This page: Fans take in a Columbus Clippers game at Huntington Park. Opposite page, from left: *Navstar '92,* three metallic sails by Stephen Canetto, graces the grounds of the Franklin Conservatory; joggers and strollers enjoy the fountains and greenery of Scioto Mile.

and improve the quality of life for its residents, while encouraging economic growth. Leading by example, the city has improved energy efficiency in its older facilities and requires every new city construction project to be LEED certified by the U.S. Green Building Council. The Green Spot program, which was launched in 2008, has engaged 3,500 businesses, residents, and community groups in comprehensive sustainable practices and continues to grow each year.

Columbus has become a showcase for green rehabilitation. The Lazarus Building, a downtown Columbus landmark that opened in 1909, is among the nation's largest green rehabilitations. More than 75 percent of the materials removed from the former department store were recycled to transform the building into a premier green office space. The lobby combines the elegant art deco style of the 1930s with 21st-century energy efficiency, while the roof is a living garden that keeps the building cool in summer and provides storm water management. Winner of the 2010 Columbus Landmarks Henry L. Hunker Urban Legacy Award, the Gold LEED-certified building houses the Columbus Chamber of Commerce, the City of Columbus and Franklin County Economic Development departments, the Ohio EPA, and other organizations.

Golfing great Jack Nicklaus, Columbus' most famous native son, won 18 major PGA championships, a record that is still intact. His extraordinary career is celebrated at the Jack Nicklaus Museum, which features memorabilia and interactive exhibits. Golden Bear wannabes can tee up at the many golf courses found throughout the area.

A former housing project that was redeveloped in 2008 became the site for Greenview Estates, the city's first sustainable residential neighborhood. A unique partnership between city, state, and private entities, Greenview consists of 30 planned single-family homes, which offer 1,200 to 1,800 square feet of living area. Energy Star-rated and Home Energy Ratings System (HERS)-compliant, this project was part of the Mayor's Get Green Columbus initiative. "We are building neighborhoods in innovative ways no one thought possible a few years ago," said Mayor Coleman, "and we're teaching the private sector that sustainable, energy-efficient homes in urban areas can sell."

Get Green Columbus

As the city approached its bicentennial, Mayor Michael B. Coleman identified the "3P" principles of sustainability—balancing the needs of people, planet, and profit. Mayor Coleman launched a targeted environmental initiative known as "Get Green Columbus." As part of this initiative, Columbus has adopted a number of ambitious green programs to reduce its carbon footprint

This page: The iconic Lazarus Building in downtown Columbus was renovated to be eco-friendly. Opposite page, from left: The LEED-certified Franklin County Courthouse boasts a green roof; cyclists enjoy a ride on the Olentangy/Scioto Bike Path.

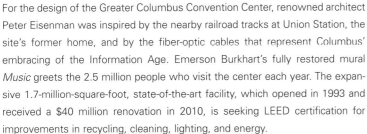

For the design of the Greater Columbus Convention Center, renowned architect Peter Eisenman was inspired by the nearby railroad tracks at Union Station, the site's former home, and by the fiber-optic cables that represent Columbus' embracing of the Information Age. Emerson Burkhart's fully restored mural *Music* greets the 2.5 million people who visit the center each year. The expansive 1.7-million-square-foot, state-of-the-art facility, which opened in 1993 and received a $40 million renovation in 2010, is seeking LEED certification for improvements in recycling, cleaning, lighting, and energy.

Another architectural showpiece is the Austin E. Knowlton School of Architecture at The Ohio State University. Dedicated in 2004, Knowlton Hall is situated at the western edge of the OSU campus, close to the river and the football stadium. At night the glass-clad library serves as a beacon for the glorious history of architecture. Mack Scogin Merrill Elam Architects was awarded the 2010 National AIA

Honor Award of Excellence for this building, which also earned the Inspiring Efficiency IMPACT Award from the Midwest Energy Efficiency Alliance.

Columbus' approach to transportation could serve as a paradigm for other cities across the nation. The city's fleet ranked in *Government Fleet Magazine*'s top 20 Best Fleets and was also named one of the greenest fleets in the nation in 2011. *Bicycling Magazine* named Columbus one of five cities to watch in the future. Columbus currently has 78.3 miles of bike routes and trails. The Bicentennial Bikeways Plan will add 36 miles of trails and 58 miles of on-street bike lanes and routes by 2015.

From green initiatives to parks and gardens, high art to high-tech innovations, Columbus provides an abundance of riches that surpasses anything dreamed of in Christopher Columbus' time.

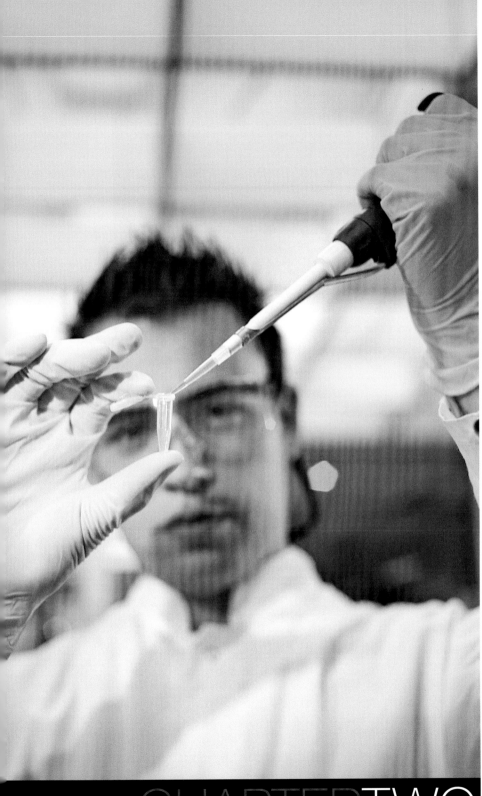

ON THE PATH TO DISCOVERY

Columbus' leadership in sustainability and high technology goes hand in glove with the quality education offered at its colleges and universities and the cutting-edge research conducted in its laboratories. With 18 four-year colleges and universities and seven two-year schools, Columbus is second only to Boston in the number of its postsecondary schools. Including graduate students, Columbus has a combined student body of more than 114,000. Tuition is low for Ohio schools, and more than 80 percent of students receive financial aid. Students can choose from numerous two- and four-year colleges, both public and private, that help prepare them for the challenges of creating a sustainable future.

Higher Education

Founded as the Ohio Agricultural and Mechanical College in 1870, The Ohio State University is the third-largest university in the nation. The Columbus campus alone has an enrollment in excess of 56,000; when research centers, regional campuses, and extension offices are factored in, the university's enrollment exceeds 64,000.

CHAPTERTWO

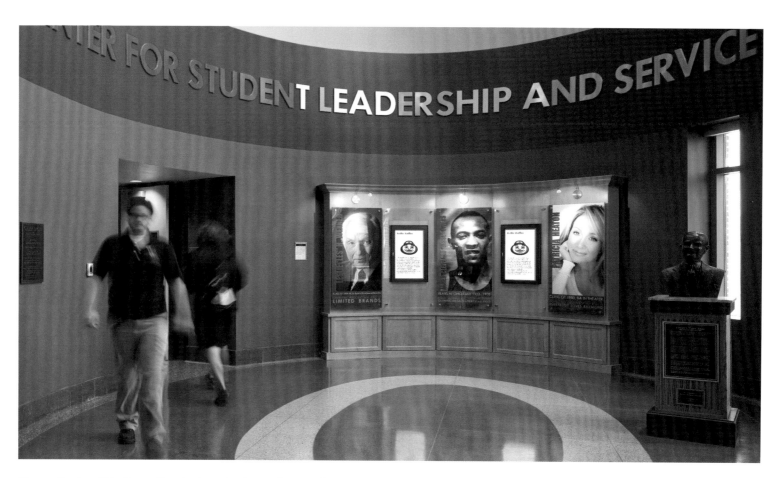

Along with size, Ohio State offers both academic excellence and value. *U.S. News & World Report* put Ohio State in its top 20 "America's Best Colleges" in 2011, while *SmartMoney* magazine ranked Ohio State at no. 11 for tuition investment, with an average return of 179 percent. Ohio State's 14 colleges offer 170 undergraduate majors and 250 master's, doctoral, and professional degrees in disciplines ranging from athletics to medicine, with concentrations that include climate change, advanced materials, and agro-biotechnology.

Ohio State's storied football tradition dates back to legendary coach Woody Hayes, who took the Buckeyes to three national championships and bested the archrival Michigan Wolverines to win 13 Big Ten conference titles. In 2002 the Buckeyes won the BCS championship and were Big Ten champions from 2005 to 2010. Ohio State's self-supporting athletics program, the largest in the nation, transferred more than $30 million to the university in fiscal year 2010–11.

While the school colors are scarlet and gray, the school is going green. The university's Ohio Union building, certified as LEED Silver by the U.S. Green Building Council, is one of two LEED-certified buildings at Ohio State. Among the student union's green features are its access to public transportation, bike racks and showers for bike commuters, and water- and energy-efficient systems indoors and out. The building was constructed using 25 percent recycled materials.

Capital University, a private, four-year school founded in 1830, is the oldest university in central Ohio and one of the nation's oldest and largest Lutheran universities. With about 3,700 undergraduate and graduate students and a student-faculty of 12 to one, Capital confers undergraduate degrees in art, music, nursing, and social work, and graduate degrees in law, business, taxation, nursing, and music.

This page: A sell-out crowd fills Ohio State Stadium for a game against the USC Trojans. Opposite page: Inspiring words greet visitors to the Ohio Union at OSU.

"Education is the most powerful weapon which you can use to change the world."

–Nelson Mandela

This page: Students enjoy a spring day at Columbus State Community College. Opposite page, from left: A stained-glass skylight graces the reading room of Ohio Wesleyan University's Slocum Hall; Otterbein University's Towers Hall, constructed in 1872, is listed on the National Register of Historic Places.

A convenient option for students who have work or family obligations, Franklin University offers undergraduate degree programs in majors ranging from accounting to Web development, and master's degrees in business, accounting, computer science, marketing, and instructional design and performance technology. Franklin's main campus is in downtown Columbus, with three satellite campuses in suburban Columbus and a fifth campus in Indianapolis, Indiana. Students can take classes online from any of Franklin's locations.

Two private universities located in the Columbus area have openly embraced sustainaibility. Otterbein University offers a sustainability program featuring an Integrated Studies class to explore global warming topics. In 2010 Ohio Wesleyan University (OWU) opened the Meek Aquatics and Recreation Center, which features such green building touches as a reflective clay tile roof and geothermal HVAC.

Two-year colleges provide students with technical skills to compete in today's demanding marketplace. Columbus State Community College (CSCC), founded in 1963 as the Columbus Area Technician's School with an enrollment of 67, now has 30,000 students at two campuses and nine off-campus centers, and in its distance learning program. Another 22,000 area residents hone their employability through CSCC's Center for Workforce Development program. Central Ohio Technical College offers associate degree and certificate programs in business, health, engineering, and public service technologies.

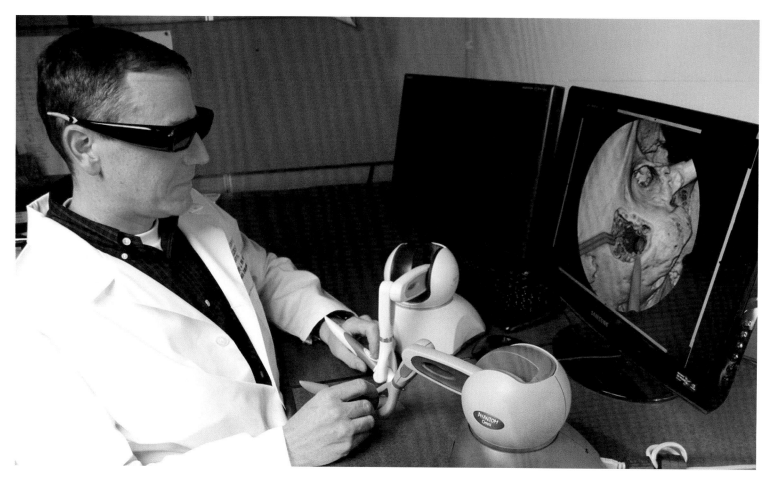

Research & Development

In 2008 *Forbes* magazine designated Columbus as no. 1 on its Top 10 Up-and-Coming Tech Cities list. Nearly a century before, in 1929, Columbus had established its bona fides as a knowledge center with the founding of the Battelle Memorial Institute, the biggest independent research and development outfit in the world. The arrival of CompuServe, the first provider of email and tech support for personal computer users, 40 years later solidified the city's reputation as a leader in technology.

Conducting $6.2 billion in research and development operations annually for American government agencies and corporations, Battelle manages the Oak

Ridge and Lawrence Livermore national laboratories, among other operations. Its numerous areas of expertise include environmental solutions that range from air quality to wastewater treatment, and a multidisciplinary approach to managing, restoring, and protecting natural resources.

Battelle's world headquarters are located on the 315 Research + Technology Corridor. A partnership among Battelle, the City of Columbus, The Ohio State University, TechColumbus, and area health care facilities, this 10,000-acre economic development and planning district is designed to be one of the largest research parks on the North American continent. Stretching between the Center for Science and Industry on the Scioto River north to OhioHealth's

facility at the west edge of Ohio State, this broad corridor contains leading hospitals, research and development laboratories, office complexes, and educational facilities.

The Ohio Supercomputer Center (OSC) provides supercomputing, research, education and training, and cyber infrastructure services to industry, the state government, and the academic community. Its applications range from studying the vastness of deep space to propelling automobiles into the future. Ohio State engineering students used the OSC's computing power to hone the aerodynamics for the Buckeye Bullet 2, the world's first research race car to be powered by hydrogen fuel cells. The car averaged a record-breaking 302.9 mph at the Bonneville Salt Flats in 2009, while an updated version, the Venturi Buckeye Bullet 2.5, reached a peak speed of 320 mph in 2010.

TechColumbus, a technology business accelerator across Kinnear Road from the OSC, offers mentoring and commercialization services free of charge to

information technology, advanced materials, and bioscience startups that are either located in central Ohio or are willing to locate here. Also on Kinnear Road, the not-for-profit Science and Technology Campus Corporation (SciTech) is a 53-acre complex of laboratory, office, warehouse, and manufacturing space dedicated to research and development. SciTech provides technology entrepreneurs with guidance and contacts at its business incubator and offers facilities at its accelerator space for companies that have achieved liftoff. A modular Science Village is in place for large firms, with another 25 acres available for future development. SciTech's affiliation with The Ohio State University allows qualifying tenants to have online access at Internet 2 speeds, with a gigabit backbone capable of supporting large-scale e-commerce Web sites.

Supported by the educated, tech-savvy workforce coming out of the colleges and universities in the Columbus area, research and development firms are taking breakthrough technology in science, medicine, and the environment from good idea to high-wage, high-growth reality.

This page: This flexible, high-tech building is the centerpiece of the SciTech campus at OSU. Opposite page: A pediatric otolaryngologist demonstrates the Virtual Temporal Bone Surgery Simulation System at the Ohio Supercomputer Center.

THE PICTURE OF HEALTH

Nationally ranked research, education, and health care institutions combine to form a powerhouse of health care in Columbus. The city's four major health care systems generate more than $4.5 billion in patient revenue and account for 31,000 central Ohio jobs. As joint founders of the Central Ohio Hospital Council, they collaborate on the city's most pressing health care concerns, such as increasing access to screenings, enhancing patient safety, and finding ways to bring the latest therapies to all patients. In addition, they support groundbreaking medical research in LEED-certified facilities that reflect a commitment to sustainability.

Three of the health systems—The Ohio State University (OSU) Medical Center, OhioHealth, and Nationwide Children's Hospital—are repeatedly named to *U.S. News & World Report*'s list of America's best hospitals. The two primary hospitals of Mount Carmel Health appear on Thomson Reuters list of the nation's top 50 hospitals for cardiovascular care.

CHAPTERTHREE

31

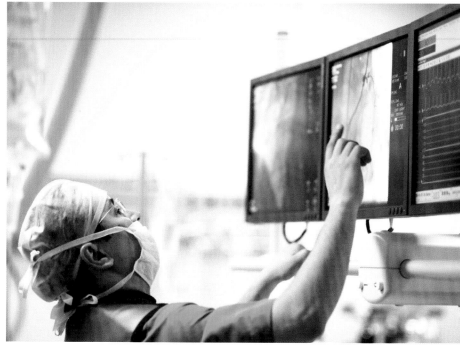

The OSU Medical Center, nationally ranked in 11 specialties by *U.S. News & world Report*, is a leading economic driver for the region, making a $2.4 billion annual impact. As an academic medical center, it swiftly translates new research into practical applications. Comprising five hospitals, more than a dozen research centers and institutes, 20 core laboratories, and a college of medicine, the center is known for six signature programs: cancer, critical care, heart, imaging, neurosciences, and transplantation.

The Ohio State University Hospital, the largest of the center's five hospitals, has been designated both a Level I Trauma Center and Level III Neonatal Intensive Care Unit and has the only adult solid-organ transplant program in central Ohio. Ohio State University Hospital East specializes in orthopedic care and family medicine in a community hospital setting. OSU Richard M. Ross Heart Hospital, a national leader in implanting ventricular assist devices (VADs), is the site of the only adult heart transplant program in central Ohio. OSU Harding Hospital offers the most comprehensive behavioral health care programs in central Ohio.

Research at the OSU Medical center has led to sophisticated new treatments for patients across the globe. Among the latest investigations is a study of Desmotoplase, a drug derived from vampire bat saliva that has been shown to dissolve blood clots in the brain for up to nine hours after a stroke—perhaps the next breakthrough for stroke patients whose treatment has been delayed past the critical three-hour window. In other research, pharmacogenomics are being used to optimize drug therapy for individuals, based on strong evidence that use of these biomarkers improves clinical outcomes. In a recent study, when the biomarker test was applied to a large number of patients requiring anti-coagulation therapy, hospitalizations dropped by nearly 30 percent.

Research funding for the OSU Medical Center had increased to $191.1 million. The Comprehensive Cancer Center received a five-year, $23 million core grant from the NCI in 2011. Growth in its research, education, and patient care capabilities created 3,700 new jobs since 2005, the largest number during this period by any employer in the region.

ProjectONE, a $1.1 billion expansion of the medical center, will add four "neighborhoods" for teaching, research, and patient care, each located in its own tower. The expanded campus, which will include a new critical care center, will provide 310,000 patients with personalized health care. The new state-of-the-art James Cancer Hospital and Solove Research Institute is a National Cancer Institute (NCI)–designated comprehensive cancer center. Patient rooms are designed with abundant natural light and access to greenery, including the new Cholis G. Ingram Spirit of Women Park. Scheduled for completion in 2014, the expansion is expected to create 6,000 direct, permanent jobs and 4,000 indirect jobs, and generate $1.7 billion in added revenue for the state economy.

The Mount Carmel Health system focuses on research, education, and health care through its four hospitals, outpatient and urgent care centers, six postgraduate physician residency programs, and the Mount Carmel College of Nursing, the state's fourth largest baccalaureate nursing degree program.

Mount Carmel Health is a leader in minimally invasive technology, offering more than 40 such procedures in eight specialties—heart, colorectal, ear/nose/throat (ENT), general surgery, gynecology, thoracic and lung, urology, and kidney. The research, application, and training in minimally invasive procedures are centrally coordinated through a dedicated institute. Mount Carmel Health also recently opened a new Heart Failure Center in downtown Columbus, which joins its two others in Westerville and on Columbus's east side.

Mount Carmel West, the flagship facility and a Level II trauma center, is a major clinical teaching site for The Ohio State University and Wright State University Colleges of Medicine. Mount Carmel East is home to new heart and maternity centers. These facilities were the first in Columbus to offer bronchial thermoplasty, a new surgery for hard-to-treat asthma patients. The procedure involves threading a small catheter through the trachea into a lung, where the tip of the device burns away smooth muscle that contributes to constriction of the airways. In clinical trials for this procedure, severe asthma flare-ups decreased by one-third and emergency department visits by 85 percent.

Consistently named hospital of choice by central Ohio residents, Riverside Methodist is part of OhioHealth, a faith-based family of 8 community hospitals and more than 40 care sites. Riverside's heart and vascular specialists are participating in a groundbreaking trial of Medtronic's CoreValve System under the direction of the OhioHealth Research and Innovation Institute. Riverside is also participating in an international trial for treating abdominal aortic aneurysms via a new procedure in which a small catheter containing a NASA–designed polymer is inserted, filling the lining of the graft to fit the patient.

Grant Medical Center, another OhioHealth hospital, is recognized nationally for heart, vascular, and trauma care, robotic and minimally invasive surgery, and the neurosciences. A Level I Trauma Center, Grant offers a dedicated Brain and Spine Intensive Care Unit and neuro-rehabilitation program to facilitate the recovery of patients suffering complex brain injuries. Doctors Hospital is one of the state's premier osteopathic teaching institutions.

This page: Entrance to Riverside Women's Center. Opposite page, from left: The Ohio State University Medical Center; a cardiologist checks an LCD screen while inserting a stent.

This page: A scientist examines a specimen under a microscope. Opposite page, from left: Surgeons perform an intricate procedure;

pediatrician at Columbus Children's Hospital examines a young patient.

One of the nation's largest and most comprehensive pediatric hospitals and a top 10 NIH-funded pediatric research institute also serves Columbus—and the world: Nationwide Children's Hospital. *U.S. News & World Report* ranked Nationwide as one of the top 10 pediatric hospitals in the country for gastroenterology and cardiology/heart surgery, and one of the top 50 in cancer, diabetes/endocrinology, neonatology, nephrology, neurology/neurosurgery, orthopedics, pulmonology, and urology. A teaching hospital, Nationwide is home to the Department of Pediatrics of the Ohio State University College of Medicine.

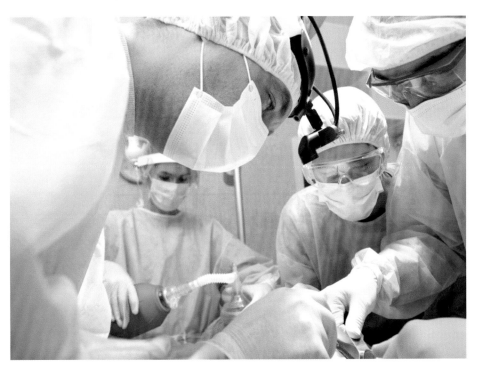

In early 2011 Nationwide was accepted into the Neonatal Research Network, a group of 18 elite research centers across the country dedicated to studying neonatal medicine. The network, developed by the National Institute of Child Health and Development, focuses on improving the care and outcome of these newborns.

Researchers at Nationwide are changing the face of pediatric medicine. In a recent breakthrough, a team found that two new small-molecule inhibitors showed promise in blocking a protein linked to osteosarcoma, the most common malignant bone tumor. The inhibitors may provide a new, nontoxic treatment for the deadly tumors, which are currently treated with a combination of toxic chemotherapy and aggressive surgical resection.

Nationwide's new, $93 million hospital is slated to open in 2012. Adding more than 2.4 million square feet to the campus, the facility will feature a 12-story patient tower incorporating the latest advancements in family-centered medicine. An emergency room will occupy the ground level, and cancer care facilities, located on the top floor, will offer chemotherapy patients breathtaking views of the city. Six acres of trees, plants, and paths will be added to Livingston Park, the existing nine-acre hospital campus.

The Research Institute is also on schedule for a new building in 2012. Research III, a six-story, LEED-certified facility, will house the Battelle Center for Mathematical Medicine, the Center for Vascular and Pulmonary Research, and the Center for Perinatal Research. The new building will support 680 new research jobs in and bring Nationwide's dedicated pediatric research space to more than 500,000 square feet. Plans call for at least one additional research building by 2025.

Life Sciences Research and Products

Columbus has attracted global companies that provide important research, products, and scientific data for the health care and life sciences fields. CAS (for Chemical Abstracts Service), a division of the American Chemical Society, is a world authority on chemical data. Its databases, which are curated by scientists and contain vast stores of information on chemicals, are relied upon by universities, governments, patent offices, and chemical and pharmaceutical companies around the world.

Battelle, the world's largest independent research organization, applies science and technology to the complex challenges of human health, pioneering advances for mankind. A subsidiary in Columbus, Battelle Medical Device Solutions develops such cutting-edge tools as an enteral feeding pump for the

Columbus-based Ross Products division of Abbott Laboratories and the Neo2000™ surgical cancer detection system for Neoprobe, a world leader in gamma detection.

Roxane Laboratories was founded in 1885 as the Columbus Pharmacal Company in downtown Columbus, taking its present name after German pharmaceutical manufacturer Boehringer Ingelheim bought it in 1978. The company and its 500,000-square-foot manufacturing and laboratory affiliate, Boehringer Ingelheim Roxane, produce and market innovative products for a wide range of clinical applications, from cardiovascular to oncology.

Cardinal Health, a $103 billion Fortune 500 company founded in Columbus in 1971, provides essential medical supplies, such as gloves, surgical apparel, and fluid-management products, through its global distribution network. Medco Health Solutions, a Fortune 500 company, manages the nation's largest mail-order pharmacy operations, helping health plans to control drug costs by designing formularies and negotiating discounts with pharmaceutical companies.

Similac has become a household name in infant nutrition. Working with leading scientists through more than 280 clinical studies, Columbus-based Abbott Nutrition developed this product line, along with an extensive array of adult nutritional products.

As breakthroughs in research are translated ever more swiftly into innovative technologies and delivered seamlessly to patients, Columbus' health care sector is certain to maintain its competitive edge far into the future.

MADE IN COLUMBUS

Columbus' manufacturing and business services sectors are going green. Manufacturers are finding new ways to reduce energy and water use, increase profits, and lessen the impact on the environment, while business services are increasingly finding ways to provide insurance, banking, legal advice, and other services while recycling, reusing, and minimizing waste.

The city itself helps green businesses grow by offering brownfield remediation, property tax abatement, business loans, and grants from the Green Columbus Fund. The latter helps private businesses and nonprofits to develop LEED-certified buildings from the ground up or redevelop brownfield sites.

Designated in 2010 as the Ohio Hub of Advanced Energy Manufacturing and Storage, Columbus is ready to marshal assistance at the federal, state, and local level to help manufacturers achieve sustainability—for instance, by working to expand the Materials+Energy+Environment+Economy (ME3), a comprehensive sustainability program, to 35 more manufacturers, with an expected savings of $15.6 million a year.

CHAPTERFOUR

Extending incentives to green manufacturers creates a win-win synergy. CODA Automotive, headquartered in Los Angeles, plans to locate a plant in Columbus to produce lithium-ion cells for its electric vehicles. The new plant is expected to invest $657 million in a former manufacturing site and create 1,000 jobs. "This can be a transformational project for our community as we leverage clean manufacturing into the future," said Alex Fischer, President & CEO, The Columbus Partnership.

CODA would be joining a distinguished list of automotive and steel manufacturers in the Columbus area. Commercial Vehicle Group (CVG) provides seats, mirrors, cabs, and interior trim for heavy trucks, military vehicles, and commercial transport, along with electrical and pneumatic systems and safety accessories. TS Tech North America designs comfortable, high-quality automobile seats and interiors. Worthington Industries, a value-added steel processor, is also a leader in manufactured metal products, including pressure cylinders and metal framing. A Y Manufacturing makes Honda sunroofs and coated metal parts. Venturi North America, a new company that will be headquartered at The Ohio State University, plans to design, engineer, and produce electric vehicles for specialty markets.

Among the Columbus companies that have found it is easy being green are Weisenbach Specialty Printing and Momentive. Weisenbach, which began producing novelty buttons from recycled material in the mid 1980s, switched to all-soy inks in 1989, uses patented funnels and spouts to capture reusable fluids, and partners with wildlife centers and aquariums to gather plastic beverage caps for recycling. Weisenbach is a Green America Certified Green Business, a registered EPA Energy Star Partner, and a Columbus Green Spot green manufacturer. Momentive, a leading global provider of specialty chemicals and material, has taken an integrated approach to sustainability, from reducing the environmental impact of its products to improving operations in its plants to making environmental consciousness part of its corporate culture.

This page: The Venturi America High Voltage Buggy electric sports car on display at the North American International Auto Show in Detroit in 2011. Opposite page, from left: Cylinders manufactured by Worthington Industries; an electric vehicle on display at CODA Automotive's grand opening in Los Angeles in 2011.

Technology remains a key component of Columbus' recent success. ABB Group, a power and automation technologies manufacturer, produces process automation solutions, variable-speed drives, and information. Mettler Toledo, whose main U.S. office is in Columbus, builds precision instruments for laboratories in the pharmaceutical, chemical, food, and cosmetics industries. The instruments' applications range from safety solutions for chemical manufacturers to monitoring the input and output of solid-waste facilities.

The sweet taste of success is no novelty to two Columbus companies. Norse Dairy Systems (NDS), which invented the sundae cone in 1928, introduced robotics to its ice cream novelty production process in 2005 to turn out sugar cones, logo-stamped wafers for ice cream sandwiches, and a wide variety of plastic and paper cups for frozen novelties. The famous White Castle hamburger chain, headquartered in Columbus, introduced "green" food packaging in all locations, replacing the white paper sack and corrugated Crave Cases with brown paper and corrugated cases made from 100 percent recycled material.

Business Services

Columbus is home to four Fortune 500 companies—American Electric Power, Big Lots, Limited Brands, and Nationwide—whose combined revenues in 2010 came to just under $47.6 billion. Columbus is also the state capital and the seat of Franklin County. This strong commercial and government presence has attracted a support fleet of firms that offer vital services ranging from banking and insurance to telecommunications.

Numerous major financial institutions operate in Columbus. Huntington National Bank, with $52 billion in assets, is headquartered in Columbus. JPMorgan Chase, which is based in New York City and has a staggering

$2 trillion in assets, acquired Columbus' Bank One in 2004. PNC Financial Services Group, a Fortune 500 company, offers retail banking, asset management, corporate and institutional banking, and residential mortgage banking. PNC is active in the Columbus philanthropic community through its Grow Up Great and Arts Alive programs. Based in Columbus, Diamond Hill Capital Management, Inc. manages seven mutual funds, with assets under management of $8.5 billion in 2011. United Retirement Plan Consultants is a leading national provider of retirement plan design, consulting, administration, and pension actuarial services for small and medium-size businesses in key markets across the United States.

Two leading insurance companies are headquartered in Columbus. Nationwide was founded in 1926 as the Farm Bureau Mutual Automobile Insurance Company, with the aim of supplying Ohio farmers with low-cost car coverage. The company, which changed its name to Nationwide Insurance in 1955, offers a full range of products for home, auto, and business. Nationwide is headquartered in downtown Columbus, in the Nationwide Arena District. Grange Insurance, a $1 billion company also headquartered in Columbus, insures homes, businesses, and lives as well as automobiles, with independent agents writing policies in Ohio and 12 other states. By building the Audubon Center at Scioto Audubon Metro Park, Grange helped to create a "green" Columbus.

Brain Magnet

Columbus was ninth among Forbes' "biggest brain magnets" in the country in 2011. One of the attractions is Quick Solutions, which won the Small Business Commerce Association's Best of Business award for computer-integrated systems design in 2010. Another attraction is Mission Essential Personnel, the federal government's main supplier of interpreters and cultural advisors for service in Afghanistan. To get the job done, it would be hard to outdo Accenture, which provides consulting, technology, and outsourcing services to a broad spectrum of clients, from aerospace and defense contractors to state and federal agencies. Small and medium-size businesses can turn to Sequent, which offers strategic consulting and a wide range of IT solutions.

Brainpower is a key asset at Columbus' leading legal and design firms. Since 1846, the law firm of Porter Wright has represented Fortune 500 companies, railroads, and the Columbus Board of Education. The imprint of DesignGroup, a Columbus architecture firm, can be seen from the downtown skyline to the campus of The Ohio State University.

From sole proprietorships to global enterprises. Columbus offers a full range of telecommunications services for home and office. Time Warner Cable provides digital cable TV, high-speed Internet service with wireless home networking, and unlimited nationwide and local phone service. Other area Internet service providers, some of whom also offer phone and video connections, include Verizon, ISP 1, and Wow!.

Three leading retailers are headquartered in Columbus. Abercrombie & Fitch designs high-quality clothing and accessories for men and women. Big Lots is the nation's largest broadline closeout retailer. Victoria's Secret is among the leading brands of lingerie, personal care, and beauty products sold under Limited Brands.

With hard work and a vision, an entrepreneur can achieve success in the Columbus market. One such example is the Charles Penzone Family of Salons, which grew from a single salon to six locations operating under three brands catering to a variety of tastes. This thriving local business, along with numerous others, demonstrate the many opportunities to grow and succeed that abound in the Columbus area.

This page: A Norfolk Southern coal train on a night run. Opposite page: A jet plane soars above the clouds.

CROSSROADS OF COMMERCE

Ohio's extensive waterfront along America's great historic highway, the Ohio–Mississippi river system, gave the Buckeye State an early advantage as a regional economic power. Lying about halfway between Chicago and the great cities of the East Coast, Columbus remains a busy crossroads of commerce, a logistics hub that is easily accessed by planes, trucks, and trains.

Port Columbus International Airport (CMH) is central Ohio's primary passenger airport. Facilities at Port Columbus include 24-hour air-traffic control, all-weather landing capabilities, an Automated Surface Observation System (ASOS), and high-intensity runway lights. Major carriers such as USAirways, AirTran, and United fly direct from Port Columbus to the hubs at Chicago-O'Hare and Dallas–Fort Worth, as well as to various Midwest and East Coast cities, including New York. Port Columbus also offers direct flights to Los Angeles, Denver, and Phoenix, and—earning its international designation—Toronto, Ontario, and seasonally to Cancun, Mexico.

The Columbus Regional Airport Authority, which administers Port Columbus, also administers Rickenbacker International Airport (LCK) in southern Franklin County. Although Rickenbacker serves private and business passenger planes, it is primarily a high-volume cargo airport. The former Air Force base in equipped with a Category I & II all-weather landing system, an Automated Weather Observation System (AWOS-3), and round-the-clock air-traffic control.

CHAPTERFIVE

In 2008, mindful of the need to save both energy and money, the Columbus Regional Airport Authority began conservation measures designed to reduce energy consumption by about 30 percent, resulting in savings of around $7 million over 10 years. Measures include installing condensing boilers and upgrading energy management systems at Port Columbus. Other possible energy-saving measures include converting chilled water, hot water, and air handling systems to variable volume systems.

Public general aviation airports in the Columbus region include Ohio State University Airport northwest of downtown; Bolton Field, southwest of the city;

and Delaware Municipal Airport in the nearby city of Delaware. For busy executives who want the convenience and luxury of traveling in a corporate jet without the expense and hassles of owning one, NetJets offers fractional ownership and rentals of private business aircraft, with costs and fees varying according to size.

Class I rail carriers CSX and Norfolk Southern provide heavy and bulk freight service to Columbus. CSX operates three lines converging from the north on Columbus, where they combine to form the Northern Line and head south to the Ohio River. This includes CSX's key coal line between Riverton, Kentucky,

Various regional and short lines serve Columbus as well. These include the Indiana & Ohio, which is owned by RailLines America, and the Columbus & Ohio River, which is part of the Ohio Central Railroad System.

Because of Columbus' central location in the state, most places in Ohio are less than two and a half hours away by road. Interstate 70 passes through Columbus from east to west, while I-71 bisects the city from north to south. I-270, a belt-way known locally as the Outerbelt, encircles the metropolitan area, while I-670, or the Innerbelt, passes through town to connect I-270 with I-70.

and Toledo. Norfolk Southern (NS) also runs coal through Columbus, where its Columbus and Sandusky intermodal lines meet. NS's Dayton line connects Columbus with Dayton and Cincinnati to the southwest, while its West Virginia single-track secondary line runs down to Charleston, West Virginia. In August 2010, Norfolk Southern linked its intermodal container-transfer terminal near Rickenbacker International Airport directly with the busy seaport at Norfolk, Virginia, via its Heartland Corridor. The rail corridor allows double-stacked cars to pass through the tunnels of West Virginia's rugged hill country rather than go the long way around through Maryland and Pennsylvania, saving 233 miles and a day's travel time. The transfer terminal volume of about 200,000 containers a year is expected to as much as double, making Columbus the go-to terminal for container traffic in the region.

This page, from left: Bolton Field services the Columbus area; I-70 is a major Columbus transportation artery. Opposite page: A helicopter touches down at OSU Airport.

This page: The Central Ohio Transite Authority (COTA) building was upgraded to qualify for LEED certification. Opposite page, from left: This new COTA hybrid-electric bus is helping to make Columbus greener; a Columbus cyclist hits the speed of life.

Several U.S. routes serve the city as well. U.S. 40 runs east to west through the city along Main and Broad streets. U.S. 23 runs through town en route to Jacksonville, Florida, in the south and Mackinaw City, Michigan, in the north, while U.S. 33, connects Columbus with Indiana and Virginia.

Columbus is expanding its green methods of moving goods and people. The Central Ohio Transportation Authority COTA, which recently added six environment-friendly electric-diesel buses to its fleet, is seeking Silver LEED Certification for renovations at its downtown administrative offices, its Fields Avenue facility, and its newly built paratransit facility. Benefits include reducing

greenhouse gas emissions and energy consumption, improving air quality, and increasing economic competitiveness.

Bicyclists are pedaling in greater numbers through the streets of Columbus. In 2008 the city council adopted the Columbus Bicentennial Bikeways Plan, an ambitious, 20-year project to add 538 miles of bikeways to the 50 miles already in place. As a result, neighborhoods and business districts will be connected with city and county parks and bikeways.

The University Area Enrichment Association encourages bicycle ridership through its volunteer-run Pedal Instead program. Developed by Mayor Coleman's Green Team, the program provides safe, supervised bike parking at festivals and events. In 2009 alone Pedal Instead helped save an estimated 2,771 gallons of gas and kept 41,425 pounds of CO_2 out of the air. There was even a valuable side benefit—participants in the program got about 5,800 hours of exercise.

Sustainable Energy

The City of Columbus is enthusiastically adopting green methods of tracking, reusing, and generating energy. Public buildings are being retrofitted with energy-efficient lighting, replacing pumps, and adding automated control systems. The city is also buying energy-efficient computers, upgrading wastewater treatment facilities, and retrofitting traffic signals and streetlights. Energy Star software is being used to compare energy use among municipal facilities and to compare those figures to national averages. Biogas recovered from the Franklin County Landfill is being used to generate fuel at a Compressed Natural Gas station. Power is even being generated underground at a golf course on the site of the old Franklin landfill.

The Columbus Green Fleet Action Plan is helping to reduce the fuel consumption and emissions of the municipal fleet. Of the 95 new on-road vehicles the City purchased by mid-2010, 76 are considered "green"— hybrid, electric, flex fuel, natural gas, CNG, or equipped with DPFs or engine heaters. All diesel fuel purchased by the city was targeted to be biodiesel by the end of 2011.

In addition to conserving energy, the city and local businesses are tapping alternative energy sources to power its way into the future. Through an agreement with Tipping Point Renewable Energy, a half-megawatt solar photovoltaic system on the roof of the Fleet Management Facility will generate an

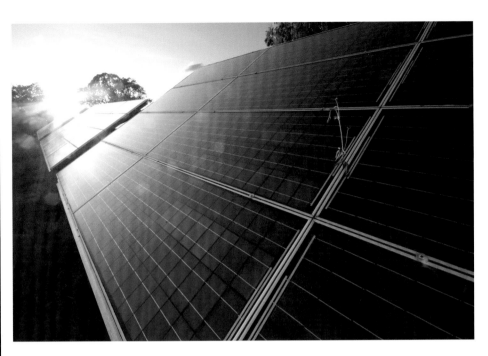

estimated 625,000 kWh of electricity each year. Bacteria is being used to break down sludge and other waste products, generating enough electricity to power 725 homes each year. A 150-foot wind generator at a local Subaru dealership produces 150,000 kWh a year, enough to power approximately six homes.

Columbus and surrounding communities still rely on traditional sources of energy. Natural gas for commercial, industrial, and residential use is supplied primarily by Columbia Gas of Ohio, the state's largest natural gas utility. Serving about 1.4 million customers, of whom about 1.3 million are residential consumers, it covers a 25,400-square-mile territory encompassing most of the state.

American Electric Power (AEP) provides electricity to its approximately 5.3 million retail customers. AEP presides over 39,900 megawatts of generating capacity and 200,000 miles of distribution lines from its hexagonal headquarters tower overlooking the Scioto River in downtown Columbus. One of the largest generators of electrical power in the United States, AEP supplies about 10 percent of the electricity consumed in the central and eastern United States and eastern Canada, operating regional utilities in 11 states, from Texas to the Great Lakes.

AEP, which derived about 7 percent of its generating capacity from wind, hydro, and solar in 2010, will seek to increase its reliance on alternative fuels. Under the State of Ohio's aggressive alternative energy policy, at least 12.5 percent of the electricity generated by utilities must come from alternative sources by 2012. AEP Ohio's gridSMART program offers rebates and cost incentives to encourage customers to use solar panels and wind turbines to generate their own electricity.

By developing alternative energy sources, conserving energy in municipal government, and encouraging citizens to take public transportation or bicycle to work, Columbus is striving to become the greenest city in the nation.

This page, from left: Energy comes from a variety of sources, from a row of solar panels to gas burners. Opposite page: High-voltage power lines provide power to businesses and residences in the Columbus area.

PARTNERS IN PROGRESS:
PROFILES OF COMPANIES AND ORGANIZATIONS

PARTTWO

PROFILES OF COMPANIES AND ORGANIZATIONS

Banking and Financial Services

The PNC Financial Services Group, Inc.

One of the nation's leading providers of financial services, this Fortune 200 company has a wide national footprint and yet remains committed to serving local customers and the communities in which it is established.

Services for Financial Success

PNC Bank offers its clients the knowledge, resources, and financial solutions they need to succeed. It provides some five million customers with a wealth of deposit, lending, cash management, and investment services, whether at one of its 2,400 branches or 6,600 ATMs or online. PNC's Virtual Wallet SM solution has been called "one of the boldest enhancements" in online banking by the international strategy consulting firm Celent. It provides a high-definition online view of a client's accounts and includes such features as online bill pay, a wish list, a savings engine, and a high-yield savings account.

PNC's Asset Management Group provides trust, private banking, tailored investments, and brokerage services to affluent individuals and families, while its Institutional Investments division serves as investment manager and trustee to businesses, retirement plans, and not-for-profit organizations. PNC is ranked by Barron's as among the nation's top 10 largest bank-held wealth managers.

The leading syndicator of middle-market loan transactions in the Northeast, PNC serves this segment through its Corporate and Institutional Banking division with treasury management, capital markets, and international banking services. The division also includes among its clients more than a third of Fortune 500 companies as well as thousands of real estate, education, health care, government, and not-for-profit institutions.

PNC also is part owner of BlackRock, providing institutional and individual investors with a variety of investment products.

Deep Community Roots

Since acquiring National City Corporation in 2009, PNC continues to grow with the central Ohio community through philanthropic outreach, economic development, and the volunteer efforts of its employees. In central Ohio, nearly $2 million has been granted to local partners through The PNC Foundation's Grow Up Great and Arts Alive endeavors.

PNC's signature philanthropic program, Grow Up Great, has been extended by $250 million over an additional 10 years to help prepare children from birth to age five—with a focus on underserved children—for success in school and life. And just as Grow Up Great provides children a solid foundation for success, PNC Arts Alive enriches the local economy by challenging local arts

This page, from left:
A PNC bank branch;
the "Living Wall" at PNC
corporate headquarters.

organizations to make the arts more accessible by expanding audience participation and engagement in new and innovative ways.

Through its community development banking group, PNC boosts the quality of life in lower-income neighborhoods through affordable housing, economic revitalization, and customized financial solutions and education. PNC remains true to the strategies and policies that have made it both a global financial leader and a good local corporate neighbor.

PNC's nationally recognized commitment to green building has enabled it to lower costs and increase efficiency and productivity as well as improve the health and vitality of the communities where people live, work, and play. The company's efforts have been recognized by the Urban Land Institute when it honored PNC among nine winners worldwide of Sustainable Cities Awards.

With more than 100 buildings certified by the U.S. Green Building Council, PNC has more newly constructed buildings certified than any other company on Earth.

PNC was the first major U.S. bank to design and build certified branches, dating back to 2002, and was granted a trademark for the term "Green Branch" in 2007.

More than 50 percent of each PNC Green Branch® location, including floors, wall covering, and furniture fabric, is locally manufactured or made from recycled or green materials. Using recycled and local products results in a significant savings to the company, while the pre-fabricated walls enable a new branch to open for business four to five weeks faster than a traditional branch. Energy usage is reduced 35 percent or more due to maximum of use of natural light plus the high-efficiency systems and installation.

The company also works to reduce impact on natural resources through various initiatives, such as recycling paper and computers, using environmentally friendly cleaning supplies, and offering customers online banking, which minimizes paper waste. From building Green Branch locations to recycling materials to reducing paper consumption corporate-wide by 20 percent in the past year, PNC is living its commitment to the environment and its communities.

For more information about PNC, visit www.pnc.com.

This page, from left: BalletMet students perform at a PNC ArtsAlive event; PNC awards the first of $1.5 million in Arts Alive grants to central Ohio arts groups.

Diamond Hill Capital Management, Inc.

An independent, publicly owned investment adviser based in Columbus, Ohio, Diamond Hill Capital Management, Inc. uses a disciplined, intrinsic value-based approach to investing and seeks to align its interests with those of its clients.

Inc. The company changed its name to Diamond Hill Investment Group, Inc. in 2001. Diamond Hill Capital Management, Inc. is a wholly owned subsidiary, providing investment management services through mutual funds, separate accounts, and private investment funds. Assets under management grew from $25 million at the end of 2000 to $8.6 billion at the end of 2010.

Diamond Hill invests in businesses that possess a competitive advantage, quality management, and a strong balance sheet. In their stock selection, Diamond Hill is always price conscious, investing only when the current market price is less than their estimate of the companies' underlying business value or 'intrinsic value.' To determine a company's intrinsic value, Diamond Hill's experienced analysts use a discounted cash flow methodology, projecting cash flows over a five-year period. Assessing the applicable industries and markets helps determine whether the per-share intrinsic value is likely to grow.

Above: Diamond Hill headquarters at 325 John H. McConnell Boulevard in the Arena District.

Pioneered by Benjamin Graham during the 1930s, the intrinsic value-based approach to investing was practiced with great success by Warren Buffett. As the billionaire investor famously remarked, "You simply have to behave according to what is rational, rather than according to what is fashionable." This dictum is the foundation of the investment philosophy of Diamond Hill Capital Management, Inc.

Originally organized as a broker/dealer focused on small community bank stocks in 1976, the firm was taken public in 1993 under the name The Banc Stock Group,

Collectively, employees, directors, and trustees had nearly $44 million invested in Diamond Hill strategies as of December 31, 2010. By aligning its interests with those of its clients, Diamond Hill has retained a loyal client base through challenging economic times. High standards of service, along with an unwavering commitment to excellence and integrity, assure client loyalty and satisfaction.

For more information on Diamond Hill Capital Management, visit the Web site at www.diamond-hill.com.

PROFILES OF COMPANIES AND ORGANIZATIONS
Energy and Utilities

American Electric Power

Founded in 1906, American Electric Power has been at the forefront of the electric utility industry since its inception. Throughout its history, AEP has pioneered myriad innovations and advancements in power generation and the transmission of electric energy.

One of the nation's largest electric utilities, AEP delivers electricity to nearly 5.3 million customers across an 11-state service territory that measures 200,000 square miles and extends from the Rio Grande River to Lake Michigan. AEP's size has fostered the economies of scale and efficiencies of diversity, flexibility, and advanced technology that have led to pocketbook savings for its residential, commercial, and industrial customers.

Headquartered in Columbus, Ohio, AEP ranks among the nation's largest producers of electricity with approximately 39,000 megawatts of generating capacity. Coal fuels 65 percent of this capacity, and AEP is an industry leader in pursuing technologies to burn it more cleanly. Natural gas provides 23 percent of the company's generating capacity, while hydro, wind, and solar contribute 7 percent, and nuclear energy the remaining 5 percent.

Innovation has been an AEP hallmark, beginning in 1911 with a 30-mile transmission line to connect the cities of Muncie and Marion in Indiana, and in 1917 when the company completed the nation's first long-distance transmission line, connecting a power plant in Wheeling, West Virginia, with customers in Canton, Ohio.

This tradition of innovation continues in the 21st century. In 2009 AEP completed the world's first fully integrated project to capture and store carbon dioxide (CO_2) from an existing coal-fired power plant. The project used a patented chilled ammonia carbon dioxide capture technology from Alstom of France on a 20-megawatt portion of the 1,300-megawatt Mountaineer Plant in West Virginia. The captured CO_2 was compressed and pumped into deep saline formations, roughly 1.5 miles below the Earth's surface.

By investing billions of dollars in environmental technologies—"scrubbers" and selective catalytic reduction systems—AEP has been able to reduce its emissions of sulfur dioxide and nitrogen oxides from its coal-fired power plants by 73 percent compared with 1990 levels.

To move the electricity to locations where it is needed, AEP operates the nation's largest transmission system, encompassing 39,000 miles of transmission lines. AEP was the first company in the U.S. to research, build, and operate 765,000-volt transmission lines, and today it has more than 2,000 miles of those lines in operation—more than all of the other utility companies in the nation combined.

Sustainable practices have been incorporated into all aspects of AEP's business operations, from strict compliance with federal and state environmental regulations to purchasing goods and materials from vendors that embrace sustainability. It also extends to providing support for universities and community colleges that are preparing the next generation of engineers, power plant employees, and line crew workers.

This page: American Electric Power headquarters building in Columbus, Ohio.

AEP has taken an active role in developing and increasing its utilization of renewable energy sources. The company currently has more than 1,500 megawatts of wind and solar capacity online or under contract, not including a 49.9-megawatt solar project in southeastern Ohio that has not yet received regulatory approval.

To give customers greater control over their energy usage, increase the efficiency of the electric grid and improve overall service, AEP launched its gridSMART[SM] initiative in 2007. From a technology standpoint, gridSMART incorporates a two-way communications system between the company and its customers that facilitates a more efficient use of electricity. For example, gridSMART may allow AEP to send price signals to customers so they can decide when to run home appliances. AEP Ohio is pursuing a comprehensive gridSMART project involving

110,000 smart meters. The project also features time-of-use tariffs, home energy use display devices, smart grid-enabled appliances, plug-in electric vehicles, and other advanced technologies.

AEP and its operating companies, such as AEP Ohio, have a significant impact on the economies of local communities. AEP has nearly 19,000 employees and pays $1.8 billion in annual wages. In addition, the company pays approximately $1.2 billion in taxes, including $850 million in state and local taxes. AEP provides tools and resources to help communities attract new businesses and the jobs that go with them.

The company is committed to playing an active, positive role in the communities it serves. In 2010 alone, AEP, its operating units and the AEP Foundation contributed $23.7 million to non-profit organizations to help improve people's lives.

Today, more than ever, American society is powered by electricity. And AEP is committed to providing clean, affordable, and reliable electric energy to the homes, schools, businesses, and industries in the many communities that it serves. For more information, visit www.aep.com.

This page, from left:
A 765-kV transmission
line and tower;
a SMART meter
used in AEP's
gridSMART project,

PROFILES OF COMPANIES AND ORGANIZATIONS

Health Care Services and Facilities

Cardinal Health

A leading health care services company, Cardinal Health improves the cost-effectiveness of health care by helping pharmacies, hospitals, ambulatory surgery centers, and physician offices focus on patient care while reducing costs, enhancing efficiency, and improving quality.

Headquartered in Dublin, Ohio, Cardinal Health is a $103 billion health care services company that improves the cost-effectiveness of health care. The company is an essential link in the health care value chain, helping to reduce costs, enhance efficiencies, and improve quality and safety.

This page:
Cardinal Health
headquarters in
Dublin, Ohio.

Providing pharmaceuticals and medical products to more than 60,000 locations each day, Cardinal Health is a leading manufacturer of medical and surgical products, including gloves, surgical apparel, and fluid management products.

In addition, the company supports the growing diagnostic industry by supplying medical products to clinical laboratories and operating the nation's largest network of radiopharmacies that dispense products to aid in the early diagnosis and treatment of disease.

Sustainable Business Practices

Aside from its commitment to help increase efficiencies and reduce costs for health care providers, Cardinal Health is also committed to supporting a healthy environment. As part of its environmental sustainability strategy, Cardinal Health has increased its focus on environmental health and safety (EHS) programs, including its environmental sustainability efforts. The company has adopted specific guiding principles for environmental sustainability focused on pollution prevention, energy efficiency, product packaging design for the environment, and employee and public education.

Cardinal Health is implementing a global environmental health and safety management system to ensure that its businesses are operating to globally recognized EHS standards. It used the same system to aid in developing a baseline carbon footprint to identify initiatives to conserve natural resources.

Specific to the health care arena, Cardinal Health is a founding member of the Healthcare Plastics Recycling Council, a coalition seeking to inspire and enable sustainable, cost-effective recycling solutions for plastic products and materials used in the delivery of health care. The company also is a founding corporate sponsor supporting the Practice Greenhealth Greening the Operating Room Initiative, which aims to reduce the environmental footprint of operating suites in hospitals across the country.

Cardinal Health is also helping health care providers reduce the amount of packaging used for and waste generated with surgical procedures through its Presource®

Procedure Packs, which consolidate individual supplies into procedure-specific kits. The customized kits help further decrease waste by reducing the number of unused items in a procedure. And, through its partnership with SRI/Surgical Express, Inc., the company led the industry with the introduction of its Hybrid Preference Pack™, the first sustainable surgical kitting solution that combines reusable and disposable surgical items into a single kit.

With these programs and offerings, Cardinal Health aims to continuously improve energy efficiency, increase both fleet and distribution vehicle miles per gallon, usage of raw materials, utilize more efficient packaging and reduce waste. The company's efforts recently have been recognized by both the U. S. Environmental Protection Agency (EPA) and the Dow Jones Sustainability Index.

The most highly recognized and longest-standing global sustainability index, the Dow Jones Sustainability Index uses best-in-class sustainability benchmarks to identify sustainability leaders in each industry on both a global and regional level

Cardinal Health is a partner in the U.S. EPA's Smartway program, which is devoted to increasing fleet efficiency and reducing the impact on the environment. The company recently achieved the program's highest possible score for private carrier fleet operations.

Cardinal Health is committed to implementing a world-class EHS system to ensure that its health, safety, and environmental sustainability programs are sound today and into the future. With its ongoing commitment to sustaining a healthy environment, Cardinal Health continues to evaluate options that will have a positive impact on the environment and the city's Get Green Columbus campaign. For more information, visit www.cardinal.com.

This page, from left: As the business behind health care, Cardinal Health offers a variety of products and services that help pharmacies, hospitals, physician offices, and other points of care be more efficient and cost-effective in treating patients. Cardinal Health operates one of the most efficient supply chains in the health care industry, delivering critical medication and medical supplies to more than 60,000 locations each day.

OhioHealth

OhioHealth has a long history of delivering on its mission to improve the health of those it serves. A faith-based, not-for-profit family of leading health care providers, OhioHealth is the largest health system in central Ohio. What started as a single hospital in 1891 has grown into a system of providers with collective strengths and specialties that together make up a complete array of high-quality care and services for the community.

Many people know OhioHealth's central Ohio hospitals by name: Riverside Methodist Hospital, Grant Medical Center, Doctors Hospital, Grady Memorial Hospital, Dublin Methodist Hospital. What they may not know, however, is that no matter which facility or service patients choose within the OhioHealth system—whether it is home health, an OhioHealth Neighborhood Care center, or a hospital—they have access to the most advanced technologies and most knowledgeable physicians and associates.

"All members of our community deserve access to high-quality health care services," says Dave Blom, OhioHealth's president and chief executive officer. As a not-for-profit health system, we have grown to provide the care our community members need close to where they live, and developed programs and services that help them achieve their best health."

From providing the most advanced, world-class care for patients with acute illnesses like heart disease or cancer, to offering preventive care and health and wellness programs, OhioHealth is committed to providing the highest-quality care. In 2011, for the third year in a row, OhioHealth was named one of the top 10 health systems in the country for clinical performance by Thomson Reuters —a further reflection of the quality and value it provides.

This page: OhioHealth staff members are committed to providing the highest-quality health care.

With eight member hospitals, including five in central Ohio and three in the region, more than 40 care sites, and countless programs and services that deliver the highest-quality care and service to its patients and visitors, OhioHealth is more than a health system, it is a belief system. Together, OhioHealth's more than 16,000 associates, 2,000 physicians and 3,000 volunteers, plus the patients, families, and communities it serves, believe in the power of their shared strength—the power of WE.

Delivering Value and Improving Health

One of the most tangible measures of OhioHealth's value to the community is the amount of community benefit it provides annually. Even in challenging economic times, OhioHealth has succeeded in fulfilling its health ministry mission and providing responsible stewardship of community health care dollars.

In Fiscal Year 2010 (July 2009 to June 2010), OhioHealth provided $191 million in Community Benefit—a $22.9 million increase over the previous year.

OhioHealth's Community Benefit includes $81.2 million in charity care, $35.1 million in net unreimbursed cost of medical education, and $2 million in community health services, just to name a few of the ways OhioHealth brings value to the community.

Every dollar OhioHealth earns is reinvested in the communities it serves to improve quality of care and enhance service to patients and families. Instead of paying dividends to shareholders or owners, OhioHealth uses its earnings to provide a wide array of community benefits, including subsidizing essential community health services such as trauma centers, poison control, or psychiatric service that some patients may not otherwise be able to pay for on their own.

"There is nothing more important than the health of our community members," says Blom. "Because we work together as a family of health care providers to be stewards of our resources, we are able to deliver on our commitment to the communities we serve and reinvest in community health in a number of ways that make a significant impact."

Additionally, OhioHealth supports a broad range of vital community outreach services, with particular emphasis on the most vulnerable and historically underserved community members. Through investing in research, innovation and technology, and medical education and training, OhioHealth works to advance medical knowledge and support a strong network of highly skilled health care professionals in central Ohio who provide the care needed to keep the community healthy.

A Leader in the Future of the Community

Employing 16,000 associates and working with 2,000 physician partners, OhioHealth is an economic driver in central Ohio. As a large organization in the community, it is an important part of the strength of the local economy, creating a substantial economic impact.

OhioHealth's belief in the power of WE is the driving force in how it cares for the health of those it serves. Bringing together the collective strengths and specialties of the people and facilities that make up the system allows OhioHealth to do more for more people—and to make the community strong, vital, healthy, and whole.

As OhioHealth continues to grow, its focus on delivering the highest-quality care at the lowest cost will be essential for the health of its patients and the future of the community.

WE includes the patients and community members who trust OhioHealth physicians and associates to care for them and those they love; with them, OhioHealth is working to make the community healthier. And that is an invaluable investment in the future of central Ohio. www.ohiohealth.com.

This page: OhioHealth patients have access to the most advanced technologies and most knowledgeable physicians and associates.

The Ohio State University Medical Center

But for Ohio State, central Ohioans would not have access to world-class health care. Committed to improving people's lives through innovation in research, education, and patient care, The Ohio State University Medical Center is shaping the future of medicine by creating and applying new knowledge and personalizing health care to meet the needs of each individual.

Ohio State continues to pursue clinical excellence and national recognition for research in every area of medicine, particularly in its six Signature Programs—Cancer, Critical Care, Heart, Imaging, Neurosciences, and Transplantation.

In 2011 Ohio State's Health System recorded more than one million patient interactions, including more than 56,000 hospital admissions and more than 120,000 Emergency Department visits. The number of employees has nearly doubled in size over the last 10 years, growing from 9,000 to nearly 17,000. Of the 558 local physicians on the 2011-2012 "Best Doctors in America" list, 483 (87 percent) are Ohio State faculty. Seven current faculty members are also members of the prestigious Institute of Medicine and National Academy of Sciences.

Ohio State supports more than 1,000 active research studies in virtually every medical specialty, incorporating more than 20 research centers and institutes and 25 core research laboratories. Total research funding has more than doubled in the last five years, and Ohio State is a major recipient of grants from Ohio's Third Frontier research program. In a time of decreasing federal funds for research nationwide, Ohio State's research funding from the National Institutes of Health has increased from $88.9 million in 2006 to $113 million in 2011. Ohio State's Comprehensive Cancer Center, one of only 41 cancer centers designated by the National Cancer Institute, received a five-year, $23 million core grant renewal from the NCI to support its broad range of clinical, research, and educational programs.

U.S.News & World Report has included Ohio State on its list of "America's Best Hospitals" for nearly two decades, singling out 11 specialties in 2011 for high-quality care, successful outcomes, and reputation for excellence. One of only 10 academic medical centers in the country to receive University HealthSystem Consortium's 2011 Quality Leadership Award, Ohio State was the first hospital in central Ohio to achieve Magnet® status and redesignation for nursing excellence. Ohio State is one of the nation's leading health care innovators, developing pioneering treatments for Parkinson's disease and novel cancer drugs in clinical trials.

This page: The new James Cancer Hospital is opening in 2014.

P4 Medicine

Using advances in genomics and molecular diagnostics, Ohio State is transforming health care delivery to provide more precise, cost-effective, and higher-quality health care for patients—a revolutionary approach called P4 Medicine. P4 Medicine is more predictive, preventive, personalized, and participatory. Treatments are designed to accommodate each patient's genetic, environmental, behavioral, and cultural factors, and personalized health management tools help predict and prevent disease instead of merely treating the symptoms. P4 Medicine also encourages patients to actively participate in the management of their own care.

When completed in 2014, the new 20-story, 276-bed James Cancer Hospital and Solove Research Institute will be a working model of P4 medicine, housing state-of-the-art facilities that provide access to high-quality medical care for significantly more patients and families.

A Matter of Degree

The Ohio State University College of Medicine ranks among "America's Best Graduate Schools" according to *U.S.News & World Report*.

Ohio State is one of the few universities in the world to offer five dual-medical degrees:

- MD/PhD (Medical Scientist)
- MD/MPH (Public Health)
- MD/MHA (Health Administration)
- MD/MBA (Business Administration)
- MD/JD (Law)

Community Support

Ohio State's Medical Center is a strong supporter of the Columbus community, providing more than $177 million in annual community benefits through charity care, outreach efforts, and other support. Ohio State is also highly regarded as a workplace of choice. Employees have named the Medical Center one of central Ohio's "Best Places to Work" in Columbus' *Business First* newspaper for five years in a row.

The New Face of Medicine

"We have lofty goals," says Medical Center CEO Dr. Steven G. Gabbe, "but if we desire to make breakthroughs in research, education, and patient care that will change the face of medicine, lofty goals are the only goals worth having."

To learn more about Ohio State's medical facilities and services, visit medicalcenter.osu.edu.

This page, left: Steven G. Gabbe, M.D., CEO, OSUMC. Above: Faculty and staff have rated Ohio State one of central Ohio's best places to work.

Boehringer Ingelheim

Striving to provide value through innovation, Boehringer Ingelheim develops new pharmaceuticals and innovative manufacturing methods to provide cutting-edge treatments for millions of people across the globe.

Today two businesses share a campus on Wilson Road in Columbus: Roxane Laboratories, Inc., a developer and marketer of generic pharmaceuticals, and Boehringer Ingelheim Roxane, Inc., a manufacturer of brand, generic, and consumer health products for Roxane Laboratories, Boehringer Ingelheim Pharmaceuticals, and various third-party customers. Employing nearly 1,200 people, these two companies share a culture of process improvement and a focus on safety, quality, and extraordinary customer service.

Boehringer Ingleheim's state-of-the-art facility in Columbus, Ohio (above left), employs nearly 1,200 skilled workers, including this laboratory scientist (above right).

In 1885, the year the Statue of Liberty arrived in New York harbor, Thomas Wells, a pharmaceutical salesman, founded the Columbus Pharmacal Company in downtown Columbus, Ohio. That same year, in Ingelheim, Germany, Albert Boehringer hired 28 people to manufacture tartaric acid salts. A century later, these two companies would join forces, reaching across the globe to improve health care for millions of people.

Through much of the 20th century, the two companies grew and strengthened, each becoming well-known for its quality medicines and innovative practices. Because of its strong reputation, Columbus Pharmacal was acquired by Philips of the Netherlands in 1959 and renamed Philips Roxane Laboratories.

In 1978 Boehringer Ingelheim Corporation, by now an international presence in the pharmaceutical industry, acquired Philips Roxane Laboratories and renamed it Roxane Laboratories, Inc.

Millions of patients across the globe benefit from the products developed at Roxane Laboratories or manufactured at Boehringer Ingelheim Roxane, including treatment options in a wide range of clinical areas, from cardiovascular to oncology.

These companies are dedicated to making a difference in their Central Ohio community. Each year they donate more than $150,000 and hundreds of volunteer hours to local organizations that promote public health, math and science education, and community well-being.

For more information on the company's products and services, visit the Web site at http://us.boehringer-ingelheim.com.

Mount Carmel

For more than 125 years, Mount Carmel has been committed to its health care mission of healing patients throughout the central Ohio community in body, mind, and spirit.

Dedicated to medical and nursing education and training, Mount Carmel has six physician medical residency programs and the Mount Carmel College of Nursing—one of the largest baccalaureate nursing programs in Ohio.

True to its mission and the commitment of its physicians, nurses and associates, Mount Carmel doesn't just provide care; it provides award-winning care. The health systems' work has received local and national recognition for quality of care, associate and patient satisfaction, community involvement, and philanthropy, including the Press Ganey Associates' Summit Award for patient satisfaction at Mount Carmel New Albany and the Achievement Citation, the Catholic Health Association's highest honor. Mount Carmel has also been designated a Fit Friendly Company by the American Hospital Association, and has received a Healthy Ohio Healthy Worksite Award from the Ohio Department of Health.

Awards, facilities, and services aside, Mount Carmel never forgets its community-benefit ministry and charitable mission. Each year, Mount Carmel provides millions of dollars in uncompensated benefits to the community. The health system is also actively engaged in the community through business, civic, and service organizations, and through its financial support of other not-for-profit organizations and social services agencies.

The health system fulfills that mission through the dedicated effort of its more than 8,700 associates and 1,500 physicians. Those efforts have allowed Mount Carmel to become the second-largest health care system in central Ohio, and, as a member of Trinity Health, part of the fourth-largest Catholic health care system in the United States.

Mount Carmel serves more than a half million patients each year through four respected hospitals—Mount Carmel East, Mount Carmel West, Mount Carmel St. Ann's and Mount Carmel New Albany—as well as through its free-standing emergency department at Diley Ridge Medical Center, outpatient facilities, physicians' offices, surgery centers, and community outreach sites.

Mount Carmel is proud of its long history of serving the central Ohio community and looks forward to its next century of outstanding care.

For more information, visit www.mountcarmelhealth.com.

Clockwise from top left: Mount Carmel East; Mount Carmel West, St. Ann's; and New Albany.

PROFILES OF COMPANIES AND ORGANIZATIONS
Higher Education

Capital University

A comprehensive, independent university grounded in the Lutheran tradition, Capital University prepares students to contribute to the world through their professional lives and personal service.

With nearly 400 full- and part-time faculty, class sizes are small, with a 12:1 student-to-faculty ratio for undergraduate students. Capital's professors excel at creating a challenging, experience-based learning environment that provides students with the tools to contribute to the world through both their professional lives and personal service.

Capital was ranked 19th among 142 top regional universities in the Midwest in the 2011 edition of *Best Colleges* by U.S. News Media Group. In *America's Best Colleges 2010*, a report by Forbes and the Center for College Affordability and Productivity, Capital was ranked in the top third of America's best colleges and universities and in the top 10 best in Ohio.

"I am pleased that, once again, Capital is recognized as one of the nation's top regional universities," said Capital President Denvy A. Bowman. "But more important is seeing our students reach their educational goals, achieve their full potential, and go on to live meaningful lives and enjoy purposeful careers. That's the real value of the Capital degree."

Undergraduate Education

Students with majors from the School of Humanities become writers, lawyers, entrepreneurs, ministers, politicians, historians, leaders, and lifelong critical thinkers who appreciate the scope of their liberal arts education.

The School of Natural Sciences, Nursing and Health is where empirical investigation meets experience. Capital has a long history of training dedicated health care providers, researchers, engineers, computer scientists, and fitness managers who balance their classroom work with clinical and business experiences.

The Conservatory of Music and School of Communication is where the creative minds of future artists, actors, news anchors, directors, performers, sound engineers, and composers find their home. From a groundbreaking partnership

This page: Each fall, members of the freshman class pass through Memorial Gateway in a ceremony welcoming them into Capital's academic community.

Located in the Columbus suburb of Bexley, Capital is the oldest university in central Ohio. But the education offered is as relevant to the world today as it was 180 years ago—experiential, intimate, and purposeful. Capital offers a personalized learning environment for undergraduate and graduate students in the arts, sciences, and professions.

Educating approximately 3,700 students each year, Capital awards undergraduate and graduate degrees in more than 60 majors and 38 minors through the Conservatory of Music and School of Communication; School of Humanities; School of Management and Leadership; School of Natural Sciences, Nursing and Health; School of Social Sciences and Education; and the Law School.

with The Recording Workshop in Chillicothe, Ohio, to study at the Zoltán Kodály Pedagogical Institute in Hungary, the Conservatory offers students opportunities to expand their musical horizons.

In the School of Management, Capital students learn from active industry professionals, gaining relevant perspectives and access to plenty of networking opportunities. Capital business students become leaders and experts in their fields of study through internships at top firms and Fortune 500 corporations and in-class consulting for local businesses.

The School of Social Sciences and Education teaches students to teach others, to solve conflicts, to investigate, to think critically, and to lead by combining pre-professional preparation with liberal arts studies in fields such as education, psychology, social work, and sociology.

Outside the classroom, Capital offers more than 70 extracurricular opportunities, including academic and professional groups, arts and media clubs, Greek life, honor societies, performance and political groups, religious organizations, service groups, and student government. Athletics play a big part in many students' lives, whether it's through intramurals or one of Capital's 18 men's and women's NCAA Division III varsity teams.

Adult and Graduate Education

At Capital University, learning is a lifelong endeavor for those students driven to do more, whether they are earning an advanced degree or completing their bachelor's program.

Graduate students enroll at Capital to earn their MBA, Master of Music in Music Education, Master of Science in Nursing, Master of Arts in Education, or Juris Doctorate degrees. For those adults who want to complete their bachelor's degree, a number of majors—including social work, business, criminology, nursing and interdisciplinary studies—are available. Certificate programs in post-degree teacher licensure, accounting, paralegal, legal nurse consultant, life care planner, and Kodály are available.

The Empathy Experiment

In 2010 President Bowman introduced a new initiative called the Empathy Experiment, which explored whether empathy can be taught, and if so, whether it can be harnessed to effect social change. Over a six-week period, six Capital students immersed themselves in projects designed by community partners, challenging their assumptions about the world and empowering them to take a more active role in their communities. "The Empathy Experiment is a monumental undertaking," said Bowman. "But it has the potential to produce powerful results for our students, community, and ultimately the world around us."

For more information about the university and its degree programs, visit the Web site at www.capital.edu.

This page: At Capital, professors are passionate about teaching and take pride in knowing each of their students, who learn through hands-on experiences in the classroom as well as internships, clinical experiences, study abroad, and service-learning opportunities.

Central Ohio Technical College

Committed to its mission to meet the technical education and training needs of students and employers in the area, Central Ohio Technical College (COTC) offers associate degree and certificate programs in arts and sciences; business, engineering and information technologies; health sciences; and public safety technologies.

In Ohio's economy, the fastest-growing job categories are those that require at least an associate degree. Central Ohio Technical College provides students with the technical skills and academic rigor that employers require to compete in today's demanding, global marketplace.

Established in 1971, COTC formed a solid and unique partnership with The Ohio State University at Newark as they developed the 177-acre Newark campus, about 40 miles east of Columbus. Viewed as a model for collaboration by the state of Ohio, this partnership provides financial efficiency, academic quality, service and convenience for students as well as the broader community.

With multiple campus locations, including Newark, Coshocton, Knox, and Pataskala, Central Ohio Technical College serves more than 4,500 students throughout Ohio and beyond. They average 28 years of age, and about 60 percent are part-time students. In 2011 a full 15 percent of COTC students were taking classes completely online. COTC students enjoy a full menu of social, athletic, arts, and cultural activities on campus.

Each academic program includes general education courses that are essential for the education of every student. All four full-service COTC campuses are equipped with state-of-the-art labs and other resources needed for today's technological fields. Throughout their academic training, students acquire the ability to communicate clearly and effectively through various methods, think critically and solve problems, employ mathematical skills

quickly and accurately, and, most important, obtain rewarding employment.

Central Ohio Technical College uses a learning management system to support online, hybrid, and face-to-face courses. COTC's online Business Management degree is designed to provide all aspects of the student's education, from orientation to graduation, in an online format.

COTC faculty members are carefully selected for their academic credentials as well as for their actual work experience in technical fields. The faculty and administrators are continually evaluating the technical and general education curricula to ensure that the college is meeting the employment needs of central Ohio. Advisory committees composed of professionals, labor representatives, and others play an important role in this process.

The Center for Academic Success, found on all four campuses, includes a Communications Resource Center (CRC) and Math Lab, augmented with online support. The Education Media and Resource Center (EMRC) on the Newark campus assists Education students and faculty with academic preparation for classes, practicum resources, and research. Nursing Student Success (NSS) on the Newark and Knox campuses assists nursing students in identifying academic challenges and resources that will aid them in achieving their goals.

The John L. & Christine Warner Library and Student Center, which opened on the Newark campus in the autumn of 2008, houses the library, Student Life offices, dining services and café, bookstore, and comfortable reading and leisure spaces. The national award-winning facility has become the hub of student activity, both academic and recreational.

CENTRAL OHIO TECHNICAL COLLEGE

Newark • Coshocton • Knox • Pataskala

In keeping with its mission, COTC's Workforce Development Innovation Center (WDIC) offers customized for-college credit and not-for-college credit training and education for area businesses. These cost-effective, innovative solutions, including entrepreneurial services, are designed to meet specific business challenges. WDIC course and program development is fully integrated with the college's academic division. In addition, employers may take advantage of customized training programs offered at the employment site or at any COTC campus, among other locations.

A Bridge to the Future

More than 9,000 students have graduated from COTC, and most immediately entered the job market. Typically, nearly 90 percent of graduates are employed full-time within six months of leaving the college, and most are working in the technology fields they studied. COTC has an increasing number of partnerships and collaborative agreements with four-year institutions in Ohio, allowing graduates to continue their studies at another college or university with minimal loss of time and credit. In many cases, students involved in these partnerships have simultaneous access to the resources of both institutions.

Central Ohio Technical College developed the Associate of Arts and Associate of Science degrees to help provide pathways for students who plan to go directly into a four-year degree program in Ohio. These students can transfer seamlessly and enjoy the affordable tuition at COTC during their first two years.

COTC is committed to playing a critical role in ensuring both the success of students and the economic future of Ohio. "The institution's academic strengths, combined with the flexibility and innovation to respond to workforce needs, ensures its integral place in the economic development of the community, region, and state and as a bridge to the future for thousands of students," said COTC President Bonnie L. Coe, Ph.D.

For more information, visit www.cotc.edu.

This page, from left: Students find a wealth of engaging campus activities and organizations at COTC; the scenic Newark campus includes the state-of-the-art Warner Library.
Opposite page, from left: COTC Gateway is a customer friendly, one-stop center for student services; staff provide personal, one-on-one advising and student support.

Franklin University

Serving the needs of adult students has guided the philosophy of Franklin University for more than 100 years. Founded in Columbus in 1902 as the YMCA School of Commerce, today Franklin is the third-largest private university in Ohio, serving a diverse population of more than 11,000 students each year, from around the world.

By offering affordable tuition, flexible schedules, multiple locations, and online programs, Franklin University provides an opportunity for busy working professionals to earn college degrees and achieve their career goals.

Franklin's educational philosophy is based on Four Cornerstones: ensuring academic quality; providing access to educational opportunities; adapting to the needs of students; and responding to changes in society, professions, and the business community. Regardless of prior academic experience or financial circumstances, students are given every opportunity to meet their educational goals. Franklin's variety of instructional approaches and high-quality curricula based on real-world needs helps ensure that students will succeed both academically and professionally.

The university's Main Campus is located on 14 acres in downtown Columbus, with suburban locations in Delaware, Dublin, and Westerville. In 2009 Franklin expanded out of state, opening a location in Indianapolis. Franklin's undergraduate programs and graduate programs are available on campus and online. Eighty percent of students at Franklin earn all or a portion of their credit hours online.

In 2009 Franklin went global, establishing partnerships with the Wroclaw School of Banking in Wroclaw, Poland, and the University of St. Kliment Ohridski in Bitola, Macedonia. The university has also partnered with Okan University in Istanbul, Turkey; Mangalore University in Mangalore, India; Sichuan University in Chengdu, China; and the University of Economics in Bratislava, Slovakia. MBA classes in English are offered at Vietnam National University in Hanoi, Vietnam, and at the Modern College of Business and Science in Muscat, Oman.

Serving more than 11,000 students each year, Franklin offers associate's, bachelor's, subsequent, and master's degree programs. Undergraduate degrees are offered in a broad range of fields, from Accounting to Computer Information Science. The program recently expanded its offerings to include a B.S. in Nursing, B.S. in Information Security, and a M.S. in Instructional Designs and Performance Technology.

In 2010 Franklin University business degree programs received specialized accreditation from the International Assembly for Collegiate Business Education (IACBE), a recognition of their consistently high quality.

Franklin students augment their classroom knowledge with the real-world experience of business professionals. Franklin's Personal Development Coaching connects students with experienced Franklin graduates who are trained to provide one-on-one career coaching. Representatives from the Ohio Society of CPAs, the American Institute of CPAs, the National Association of Black Accountants, and other industry groups participate in seminars and networking events sponsored by

Founded in 1902, Franklin University has serves the needs of more than 11,000 students each year.

Franklin's Accounting Major. The Credits to the Profession program brings in accounting experts from such diverse organizations as the Columbus Zoo & Aquarium and the Columbus Blue Jackets, the city's National Hockey League team, to speak about their nontraditional accounting roles.

Students interested in earning an MBA will find they are getting top value for their dollar at Franklin University. In 2010 Franklin's MBA Program was ranked as a Best Value in Regionally Accredited Online MBAs by GetEducated.com, a consumer group that ranks online universities based on a comprehensive, independent survey of 90 regionally accredited business schools. The program's faculty is also first in its class. Dr. Doug Ross, Program Chair of the Master of Science in Marketing & Communication (MCM) and MBA programs, was named the 2010 Outstanding Marketing Educator by the Central Ohio Chapter of the American Marketing Association (AMA).

Change is inevitable, a fact that is hard-wired into Franklin's approach to education. "We monitor and anticipate societal shifts, which enables Franklin to stay in step with workplace demands through enhanced program design and expanded technology application," said Dr. David R. Decker, President. With the dramatic increase in the mobility of labor and capital in world markets and the growing reliance on technology, Franklin is committed to helping students develop the mindset and skills to adapt to change through their careers.

Franklin University puts its philosophy into action with community outreach. In 2007 the university joined the CCS Higher Education Partnership (HEP) program, a consortium linking CCS with nine Central Ohio colleges and universities and I Know I Can, a scholarship program for disadvantaged high school seniors.

From its Main Campus in downtown Columbus to the far corners of the world and online, Franklin is helping prepare students for the challenges—and opportunities—of the modern global economy. For more information, visit www.franklin.edu.

This page, from left: Adapting to the needs of students, Franklin University offers classes at multiple locations and online. Franklin's Main Campus is located on 14 acres in downtown Columbus where the Nationwide Library, Student Learning Center, Paul J. Otte Center for Student Services, Franklin Bookstore, and the Office of the Registrar are located, along with classrooms, computer labs, testing and tutoring facilities, study centers, and meeting rooms.

Ohio Wesleyan University

A small national university with a major international presence, Ohio Wesleyan University has been a leading institute of higher education in the Buckeye State since 1842, preparing students for leadership and service in a global society.

self-fund individual research projects around the world. Students flock to OWU for the opportunity to compete for one of these university-supported grants. From Brazil to Bangladesh to Borneo, and everywhere in between, students are engaged in research projects dealing with global economics, sustainability, ecology, biodiversity, water issues, and disease management, among many others.

Ohio Wesleyan students also experience the world through an extensive program of mission experiences. The university routinely fields eight to 10 teams per year, far more than most other liberal arts colleges of similar size. In recent years teams have served throughout the United States and in El Salvador, Dominica, Haiti, Honduras, and Rome, and for many students the experiences have been life-changing.

This page:
The "green"
Meek Aquatics and
Recreation Center
is Ohio Wesleyan's
newest building.

The Opposite of Ordinary

Located in Delaware, Ohio, Ohio Wesleyan has approximately 1,850 men and women undergraduates who come from nearly every state in the union and more than 50 countries throughout the world. In fact, OWU boasts one of the nation's largest percentages of international students among private liberal arts colleges.

But Ohio Wesleyan doesn't just bring students to campus; it sends them out as well. OWU students are found on six continents, participating in travel-learning experiences that are second to none. Most notable is the university's Theory-to-Practice initiative, a competitive grant program that allows students to design and

The Academic Profile

Ohio Wesleyan offers 93 majors, sequences, and courses of liberal arts and pre-professional study in 24 departments and nine interdisciplinary programs; OWU confers a Bachelor of Arts and two professional degrees: a Bachelor of Fine Arts and a Bachelor of Music. The university's outstanding pre-law, pre-medicine, pre-dentistry, pre-public administration, pre-theology, and pre-veterinary medicine programs prepare students for entry into the country's most prestigious professional schools. Offering 3-2 combined degree programs in engineering, medical technologies, optometry, and physical therapy, OWU is one of only 13 undergraduate institutions in the country to have a 3-2 engineering program with the California Institute of Technology.

OWU and the Earth

In 2008 the president of the university convened the President's Task Force on Sustainability to develop and institute strategies for creating a more environmentally friendly campus. OWU students, faculty, and administration are working together to realize these goals. In addition to coordinating the recycling program and composting, students have created an on-campus organic garden and instituted a shared bike program to cut down on automobile emissions. Residents of the Tree House, a small living unit for students, raise awareness about environmental issues, and often help initiate new "green" projects.

The administration is dedicated to sustainable, earth-friendly renovation and new construction. OWU's newest building, the Meek Aquatics and Recreation Center, features a geothermal energy system that heats and cools the building, and a heat-recovery system that heats water for the pool. The Meek Center also includes a reflective clay-tile roof as well as recycled, regional, and low-VOC (volatile organic chemical) building materials.

Ohio Wesleyan University students and faculty are engaged in large-scale collaborative ecological research coordinated by an OWU professor and involving faculty from 11 additional institutions. The National Science Foundation has awarded the coordinator and the collaborating schools a five-year grant to fund the Ecological Research as Education Network (EREN). This network develops collaborative research projects that focus on regional to continental-scale ecological issues, engaging students in authentic science while teaching them basic ecology. A continental-scale ecology course module using research data will be team-taught by scientist-educators from participating institutions, establishing an online database of collaborative data sets collected during the project.

Community Well-Being

OWU also is committed to community well-being. The university's Healthy Bishop initiative offers a continual study of how campus resources and programs can be improved to encourage recreation, fitness, and healthy lifestyles among the OWU community.

Ohio Wesleyan always has prepared its graduates for the times they are about to enter. Today the university continues that long tradition as its graduates take their places in a smaller, more interdependent, and more environmentally conscious world.

For more information on Ohio Wesleyan, visit the Web site at www.owu.edu.

This page, from left: Students gather for an event on the JAYwalk in front of OWU's Hamilton-Williams Campus Center; students work in the community garden, part of OWU's commitment to creating an environmentally friendly campus.

Otterbein University

Historically progressive. That is the hallmark of Otterbein University and those connected to this private, liberal arts university nestled in the picturesque, historic Uptown Westerville district in central Ohio.

across disciplines. Now Otterbein is helping set the national conversation for its pioneering work in experiential learning. Chosen as one of only six institutions in the country, Otterbein is poised to help others understand how to best harness the transformative power of hands-on learning through its "Five Cardinal Experiences."

Integrity, humane values, and an inherently just moral compass have guided Otterbein's progressive vision and actions—from its curriculum to its responsibilities as a member of the academic and regional communities.

Otterbein's thoughtful commitment to a sustainable future can be measured in

Since its founding in 1847, Otterbein University has been committed to providing students with an experience and an education that are progressive, innovative, and inclusive.

Otterbein is believed to be one of the first colleges in the country founded as a coeducational institution that enabled women to follow the same course of study as their male counterparts. Not only did women stand shoulder to shoulder with men as students—they also proudly served as faculty members from the school's earliest days. Otterbein is also believed to be one of the first in the nation open to students of color since its founding.

That spirit, now re-envisioned for the 21st century, finds Otterbein's curriculum nationally recognized as a model for educating the whole student. The long-standing Integrative Studies Program continues to earn high praise from national and international higher education experts for the powerful ways it integrates learning

commonly valued standards such as energy conservation, reduction of waste, and recycling materials as well as bold, comprehensive efforts such as those happening at the University's new state-of-the-art Center for Equine Studies.

The site that hosts this industry-renowned facility serves as much more than a modern home to the Equine Sciences program. The site has carefully and purposefully evolved into a living, working laboratory operating with a sustainable approach—from off-site animal waste composting, to a community garden whose crops are distributed to area service organizations thanks to the tending of Otterbein and area elementary and secondary schools, to wetland protection and research efforts. Up next, the university is seriously investigating solar energy usage opportunities.

You're invited to learn more about Otterbein's commitment to its students, its community, and its innovative sustainability efforts by visiting www.otterbein.edu.

Above, from left:
Otterbein's unique
Center for Equine Studies
program sits on 70 acres.
Otterbein students live
the "Five Cardinal
Experiences," which
include opportunities
to study abroad.

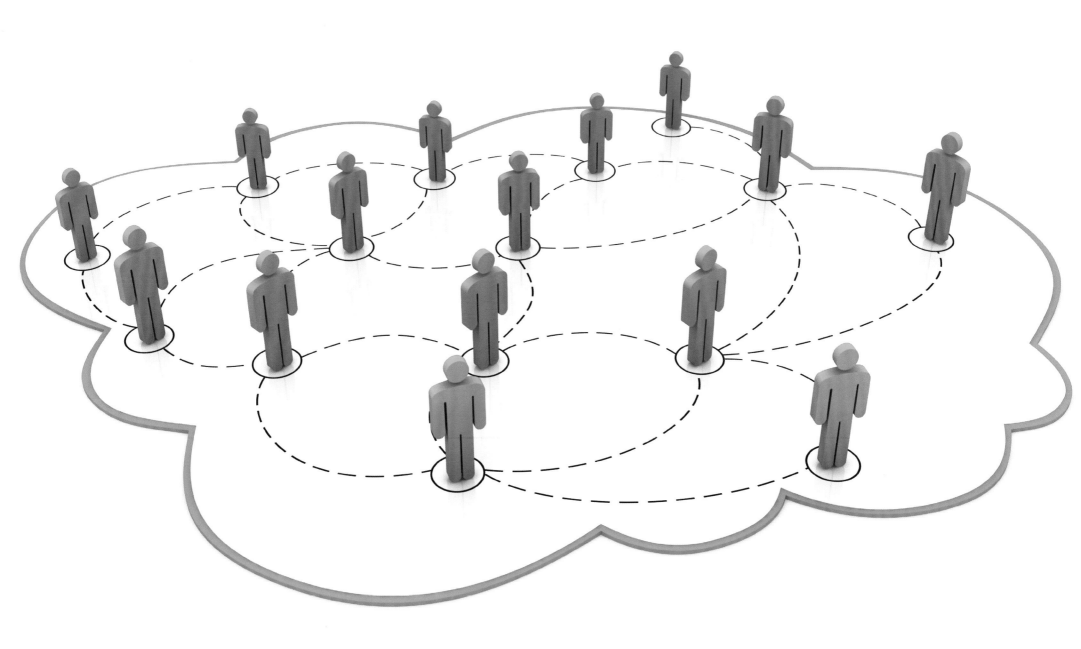

PROFILES OF COMPANIES AND ORGANIZATIONS
Information Technology

Quick Solutions

A premier IT consulting firm, Quick Solutions Inc. (QSI) provides a broad range of strategic and cost-effective services to clients operating within a vast range of industries. Quick Solutions is a leading consulting and solutions provider for numerous national companies, including Cardinal Health, Nationwide, American Electric Power, Wendy's, and BMW. QSI has a reputation of collaborating with clients to not only meet, but to exceed their needs and expectations.

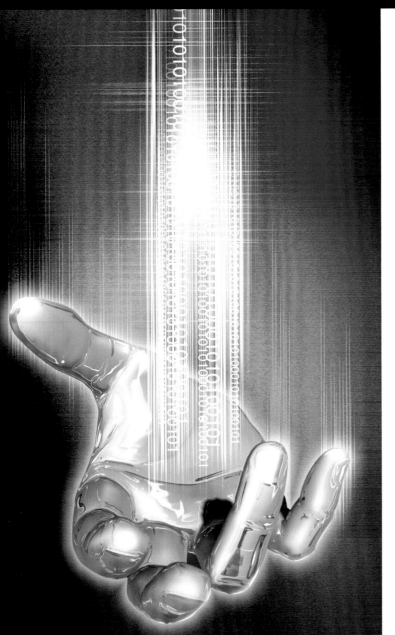

Efficient, affordable IT solutions are essential to succeeding in today's competitive global marketplace. QSI, one of the largest privately held Information Technology service providers in Ohio, offers leading edge technology services around Strategy, People, Process and Technology. Including disciplines such as Agile delivery and adoption, project management, application development, business analysis, quality assurance, IT strategy, business intelligence, creative services, infrastructure, and more. Quick Solution's client centric focus allows them to help clients utilize resources effectively to optimize results.

Founded in 1991 in response to the growing demand for Information Technology consulting services, QSI now employs more than 190 consultants at more than 70 client sites. Working within the clients' priorities, budget, and culture, QSI assists companies in developing and implementing meaningful IT strategies, and providing a clear, attainable IT roadmap that is closely aligned to their strategic business initiatives.

QSI's SureSolve™ methodology ensures that the solutions and software applications perform as intended, a holistic approach that reflects QSI's breadth and depth of engineering talent.

Gold Partner

Quick Solutions is a preferred supplier for a number of Fortune 500 companies. Applying its IT expertise, QSI helps businesses maximize their revenues by decreasing costs, reducing risk, and accelerating time to market. As a Microsoft Gold Partner, QSI is able to leverage their service offerings to meet the needs of their clients. Quick Solutions was selected from an extensive field of Microsoft partners for delivering market-leading customer solutions built on Microsoft technology, winning the Small Business Excellence Award as part of Microsoft's H2 Heartland Area Partner Awards Program. Now a Managed Partner, Quick Solutions is responsible for maintaining Microsoft expertise and implementing Microsoft-based solutions at client sites.

Quick Solutions has a reputation for providing strategic and cost-effective services to a broad range of industries, including Financial Services, Education, Retail, Energy, Manufacturing and Distribution and Public Sector agencies. QSI leverages iterative Software Development methodology, such as Agile, Scrum and Lean to deliver projects within the expected timeframe, budget, and with the intended results. The outcome is client satisfaction and success. "The Quick Solutions model allows us to complete projects on time and within budget, which is critical in satisfying our board of directors and creates a business environment where developers flourish by having realistic goals and objectives. They have not only helped us build better applications but they have helped us build a better business," stated the Chief Information, Strategy and Integration Officer of a large claims management firm.

Quick Solutions has delivered over 150 Agile projects since 2002 utilizing their SureSolve™ methodology. Their 54 years of Agile experience on the Management

Team has led to reduced costs, maximized speed to market, improved schedule and budget forecasting accuracy, and resulted in delivering the right solution. QSI partners with national Agile Thought Leaders, including Ken Schwaber of Scrum.org. This partnership makes QSI the only partner of Scrum.org in North America, and only one of four partners in the world!

Quick Solutions' ability to achieve consistent results for its clients has earned it a number of accolades. QSI was voted Best Information Technology Consultants by Columbus C.E.O. Magazine in 2009, 2010 and 2011. QSI also made the Inc. 500 list four times and the Columbus "Fast Fifty" list for five consecutive years. QSI is also an active member of the ESOP Association and TechServe Alliance.

Quick Solutions continually strives to be the destination for the best and brightest IT consultants. QSI works to attract and retain individuals committed to success and growth. In an industry that changes so rapidly, QSI fosters an atmosphere that encourages its employees to adapt by offering training, networking and educational opportunities. To acquire and retain the top industry talent, QSI has established career path models, which provide a clear path for advancement and growth within the

THINKING AGILE...
Quick Solutions' SureSolve™ methodology is faster, higher quality, and more cost effective.

organization. By investing in their people, Quick Solutions is able to deliver quality resources and value to their clients across all industries.

Community Service

Quick Solutions' employees donate their time and creativity to benefit their community. Nearly every QSI employee is involved in the community one way or another, whether it is a weekend-long event for GiveCamp, where IT leaders team up to create custom software for nonprofit organizations or participating in volunteer days, food drives, and raffles in support of the Mid-Ohio Foodbank. QSI also sponsors events for charities, including Halfway to St. Patty's Day for Cystic Fibrosis, Huntington Golf Outing for Pelotonia, Prevent Blindness Ohio Golf Outing, and the Buckeye Ranch Bash, to name a few. In the same spirit of giving, QSI employees frequently take part in speaking engagements with local user groups and several IT organizations in the area.

Throughout Quick Solutions' expansion, they have stayed true to the founding philosophy of a commitment to providing value to clients, while enriching the lives of their employees. This philosophy has formed every step of their past development and will guide their growth in the years to come.

For more information on Quick Solutions, Inc., visit quicksolutions.com or connect with them on Facebook and Twitter.

Time Warner Cable

Time Warner Cable is all about connections—connecting people and businesses with information, entertainment, and one another. With its innovative products and services such as high-definition television, enhanced TV features, high-speed data, and Digital Phone services, Time Warner Cable keeps its customers connected.

Above, from left:
The headquarters
of Time Warner Cable's
Mid-Ohio Division
on Olentangy River
Road in Columbus.
Time Warner Cable
customers enjoy
innovative products and
services such as high-
definition television and
enhanced TV features.

Innovation has been the hallmark of Time Warner Cable in central Ohio since its arrival in 1973. This commitment to innovation put Columbus in the cable history books with the debut of the nation's first interactive cable technology system, known as QUBE, in 1977. For the first time anywhere, customers could "talk back" to their televisions, vote in on-air polls, and participate in live auctions.

Today, the company's Mid-Ohio Division headquarters is an anchor of Columbus' Research and Technology Corridor, located near downtown. Built in 2007, the headquarters was the first building established on the former landfill site known as "Gowdy Field," beginning the transformation and revitalization of the area.

The headquarters is the hub of a division that employs more than 2,000 and serves nearly 600,000 customers stretching from northwest Ohio to southeast Ohio.

Innovation remains a central theme at Time Warner Cable, with new technologies being introduced and developed to give customers unsurpassed convenience and control. With revolutionary services such as Start Over, Look Back, On Demand, and Digital Video Recorder, customers are freed from the constraints of programming schedules like never before. Time Warner Cable is committed to being the company that connects its customers to the world—anytime, anywhere, from any device.

Time Warner Cable also is committed to connecting in the community through its signature philanthropy program, Connect A Million Minds, designed to inspire the next generation of problem solvers. By boosting interest in the areas of science, technology, engineering, and math, Time Warner Cable hopes to ready our youth for the challenges of the 21st century.

With its award-winning digital technology, Time Warner Cable will continue to lead the way in offering home entertainment and information choices that keep people connected. For more information, visit the Web site at www.timewarnercable.com.

PROFILES OF COMPANIES AND ORGANIZATIONS
Insurance

Grange Insurance

Born and raised in Columbus, Grange Insurance reflects the city's Middle American values, work ethic, and ambition to succeed. From its humble beginnings to its current status as a $1 billion organization, Grange is positioned to grow, diversify, and build more than ever before in its 75-plus-year history.

Like many successful companies, Grange Insurance was formed to fulfill a specific need in the market—provide more affordable auto insurance for rural drivers, who faced far fewer perils on the road than their city brethren.

Since then, Grange has remained focused on doing things just a little bit better, and effectively managing its finances to make sure the company will always be there for its customers when they experience a loss.

In fact, since beginning operations on the sixth floor of the Great Southern (now Westin) Hotel in 1935, Grange has been a trusted partner for businesses and families. Without insurance, businesses can't get off the ground, houses can't be built, and the risk of driving a car would be cost-prohibitive. Grange always has managed its business conservatively in order to maintain the financial strength and peace of mind its policyholders require from their insurance company.

Grow, Diversify, Build

Under the direction of a strong management team, Grange's plan for the future can be summed up by three simple charges: grow, diversify, and build. These goals are what guide the company's leaders and associates in their quest to build a bigger, stronger, and more financially diverse insurance provider. After all, as it was once said, "If you don't know where you're going, any road will take you there." Grange knows where its challenges lie, has already taken measures to meet them, and has a clear plan for where it's going.

That plan includes remaining an industry leader through growth. Grange looks to organically grow by enhancing and balancing out its existing businesses. In the coming years, the emphasis will be on boldly expanding the amount of commercial and life insurance coverage the company writes. At the same time, Grange will steadily expand its personal lines business, which includes insuring the autos, homes, and other property of individuals and families.

Photo: © Matthew Carbone

As an organization that sells its products only through independent insurance agents, Grange is working to deliver tailored service and sales support that will help each of its more than 3,000 agents grow their business with the company. Just as Grange can't grow without its agent partners, it also can't grow without the support of dedicated employees. The company is making a keen effort to develop, engage, equip, and reward associates to ensure that it meets its strategic growth goals.

In addition to achieving organic growth, Grange will look to acquire or affiliate with other insurance carriers that can help it fill a gap with either a different set of products it offers, a new geographic area, or both. Diversifying its business through acquisitions and affiliations will help the company spread its risk and expand into more markets.

Finally, Grange is looking to build on a long history of improving customer experience through the effective use of technology and industry-leading claims service. The company will continue to boost its operational effectiveness and better understand its policyholders and agents in order to meet their changing demands. The most successful businesses in any industry are the ones that understand what their customers need and deliver it faster and more conveniently than the competition. Grange will work to stay ahead of the curve and meet those expectations.

Committed to Independents
Since its inception, Grange has distributed its products only through independent agents. Why?

Opposite page: A part of Columbus since its founding in 1935, Grange has been an anchor for the Brewery District just south of downtown since first locating in the area at 671 South High Street in 1948.

This page: Grange Insurance celebrated its 75th anniversary in 2011 by unveiling this custom-designed piece from artist Lawrence Romorini. The art is on permanent display in the company's Innovation Center.

Left photo: Claims representative Chris Snow explains settlement paperwork to a client two days after a tornado damaged her father's home.
Right photo: Company leaders meet with Agent Advisory Board members in a breakout session.

Grange strongly believes that independent agents provide the best value and service to insurance consumers. Independent agents can choose not only from a wide variety of products, but also from various insurance companies to find the best possible insurance coverage that meets the exact needs of their customers. As small businessmen and women who live, work, and play in the communities where their offices are located, independent agents are in a position to offer the best advice and counsel to their neighbors. They know the community, the unique risks of the area, and which companies provide great service. By working with an established company like Grange, independent agents know they're recommending a company on which they and their customers can rely.

Modern Conveniences, Traditional Values

Historically, Grange has invested heavily in technology to provide service that differentiates the company from its competitors. Being fast and being accurate are important competitive advantages in the insurance industry. For example, the company utilizes technology to track storms that pass through regions with Grange policyholders. In the wake of these storms, Grange claims adjusters are able to get in contact with customers to see if they've suffered any damage—many times before the customer has even been able to call in a claim. The company's investment in technology is verified by the numerous technology awards it has received from various organizations through the years, including the most recent award, the 2011 Interface Partnership Award from Applied Systems.

Grange also has garnered numerous other prestigious awards. The company was the 2011 winner of the Eagle Award from the Independent Insurance Agents of Ohio, which recognizes the outstanding insurance company of the year. "We appreciate and recognize the cooperative effort working with Grange in promoting a vibrant insurance industry for the benefit of the Ohio consumer," said Ohio Big 'I' President Ed Wade in presenting the award.

Columbus: A Community of Choice

Grange Insurance is proud to call Columbus home, reflected in its commitment to the community. Over the years, its associates have donated millions of dollars to the United Way of Central Ohio and other charitable organizations. In addition, the "Grange Ambassadors" have volunteered hundreds of hours at community events conducted by area non-profit organizations to improve the lives of their neighbors.

Perhaps the company's largest measure of community support was its commitment to building the Grange Insurance Audubon Center at the Scioto Audubon Metro Park. Formerly a dilapidated brown field just south of Downtown Columbus, the area was filled with empty warehouses, overgrown fields, and trash. Today it is a community jewel and the first Audubon Center in the country to be built so close to the heart of a major city. In addition to the beautiful park space, riverfront, and migratory bird area, the Grange Insurance Audubon Center provides cross-curricular, nature-based education designed to improve the academic performance of students and schools in all areas for generations of students to come.

In many ways, Grange Insurance reflects the city's growth from a small, dependable entity to the vibrant, diverse, and energetic enterprise it is today. And just like the city, Grange will continue to grow toward its ultimate potential, diversify to be ever more inclusive, and build upon its solid, Middle American foundation.

As Columbus continues to thrive, Grange will continue to be an anchor around which the Brewery District can continue to develop and be an important part of the fabric of the community for years to come. For more information, visit www.grangeinsurance.com.

This page: A LEED-certified facility, the Grange Insurance Audubon Center contains classrooms, observation decks, and a multi-purpose room. Located just a mile from downtown Columbus, it will serve members of the community for generations to come.

Nationwide

Nationwide is proud to be a part of Columbus. In 1926 Nationwide began as an insurance company for farmers with unique needs. As Nationwide grew through the years, it focused on its customers and the ever-changing consumer and Central Ohio landscape.

This page: Since its founding in 1926, Nationwide has maintained its headquarters in downtown Columbus.

Nationwide Grows Up with Columbus

Today a large percentage of Nationwide's employees work in Columbus. With a culture of unity, teamwork, and dedication to service, Nationwide's associates and agents are passionate about making a difference in the lives of others in their hometown community.

Nationwide provides insurance and financial services with one simple goal: to help people protect what is most important and secure their financial futures. It offers a full range of insurance products for home, car, and business, as well as financial services to help protect customers throughout their lifetime, including retirement. These include:

• Auto, homeowners and commercial insurance
• Insurance for motorcycles, boats, vehicle fleets and mobile homes
• Traditional life and variable life insurance
• Annuities, retirement plans and mutual funds
• Checking and savings accounts, mortgages and home equity lines of credit
• Pet insurance

Nationwide's associates, agents and partners deliver this wide array of products and services with a commitment to On Your Side® service. It's how Nationwide has served customers for more than 80 years and how it will continue serving them long into the future.

Making a Difference in the Community

Through the years, Nationwide has contributed millions of dollars and countless volunteer hours to Columbus-based nonprofit organizations to save, rebuild, and enrich lives. The company, and its associates and agents, have a long-standing commitment to improving the quality of life in communities in the Central Ohio area through personal volunteerism and corporate contributions.

In recent years, Nationwide made several significant contributions to the Mid-Ohio FoodBank, United Way, and the American Red Cross of Greater Columbus. In 2006, the Nationwide Insurance Foundation donated its largest single gift, a $50 million grant, to Columbus Children's Hospital.

With a focus on community programs and emphasizing the importance of helping others, Nationwide makes its company and the Columbus community stronger, better, and healthier.

Developing New Generations of Leaders and Creating Career Opportunities

By focusing on people, Nationwide ensures it remains a vital part of the Columbus community for years to come. Nationwide creates career opportunities and recruits associates and agents who are committed to providing the best experience for Nationwide customers. Nationwide offers rotational leader development programs in several general and technical areas across the organization. These programs give leaders the opportunity to work on high-profile assignments, acquire foundational knowledge, and develop broad competencies—all to ensure future business success.

Recruiting Top Talent

Having an inclusive culture in which people feel challenged, appreciated, respected and engaged is key to Nationwide's success. Its culture promotes authenticity, innovation, and a commitment to help people reach their career goals.

Nationwide recruits highly talented individuals who thrive on developing new and creative ways to deliver its On Your Side promise to its customers. The company's goal is to develop and retain a diverse and talented workforce that represents the markets and communities it serves.

Nationwide is also involved in the city's efforts to attract and retain young talent. The company is committed to providing career opportunities that keep in the region students who graduate from Central Ohio colleges and universities. Putting a special focus on local recruitment helps fuel the city's workforce development needs now and in the future.

Nationwide believes that if its people are passionate about where they work, they'll be passionate about serving customers. That's been Nationwide's strategy for success for its entire history.

Nationwide: Growing with Columbus

Through large real estate investments over the years, Nationwide has become a cornerstone of development in downtown Columbus. Nationwide's corporate headquarters have been located downtown since its beginning. From the mid-1970s through the 1990s, it developed buildings—including its headquarters complex—that contributed to the revitalization of the northern part of downtown.

In the 2000s, the company created the Nationwide Arena District, which immediately surrounds its corporate headquarters and includes Nationwide Arena, home to the city's National Hockey League team, the Columbus Blue Jackets. The Arena District has become a vibrant commercial and residential district, as well as a focal point for entertainment. www.nationwide.com.

This page, from left: Home of the Columbus Blue Jackets, Nationwide Arena is the centerpiece of the Nationwide Arena District. Nationwide's associates and agents have a long history of volunteering for Central Ohio nonprofit organizations, including the Mid-Ohio Foodbank.

PROFILES OF COMPANIES AND ORGANIZATIONS

Management Consulting/R&D

Battelle

Battelle was founded in Columbus, Ohio, by the last will and testament of Gordon Battelle, a pioneering leader in the early days of America's steel industry. With a dedication to advancing science and technology to benefit humankind, the nonprofit trust known as Battelle began operations in 1929.

Today Battelle is the world's largest independent research and development organization, providing innovative solutions to some of society's most pressing science and technology challenges. From its headquarters in Columbus, Ohio, Battelle oversees 22,000 employees in more than 130 locations worldwide.

The Battelle philosophy is simple: Combine the best people with world-class equipment and facilities, and a culture that rewards and enables ingenuity. That way, Battelle's efforts accelerate the rate of innovation instead of simply creating new products. Embracing an established culture of continual refreshment of ideas in business operations and processes, Battelle doesn't just follow the latest trends in R&D and business management—it is a leader in developing and implementing the conditions in which new ideas and inventions can be nurtured.

Battelle systematically drives innovation in four key areas:

* Products: Through its science and technology initiatives and the R&D work it does for its clients, Battelle is a recognized leader in translating new scientific discoveries into new products and technologies in each of its core business areas.
* Processes: Battelle's process improvement teams are continually looking for ways to facilitate internal and customer communication, strengthen ties between science and industry, and automate and accelerate the innovation process.
* Business Models: Battelle is extending its reach and access to resources through collaborations and joint ventures with the private sector, international partnerships, and alternative financing options for research and facilities.
* Culture: Battelle's scientists and engineers are active participants in the wider scientific community, collaborating with partners in universities, national laboratories, and industry to drive scientific discovery. Battelle also is committed to developing the next generation of scientists and engineers through its STEM (science, technology, engineering, and math) education initiatives.

In terms of business, Battelle is organized into the following strategic areas:

Global Businesses: Battelle brings together leading scientists and engineers with the world's greatest collection of science and technology assets to develop products, systems, and services in three strategic focus areas:

* Energy, Environment, and Material Sciences
* National Security
* Health and Life Sciences

Laboratory Management: Battelle manages or co-manages six national laboratories for the U.S. Department of Energy, along with the nation's premier biological threat characterization and bioforensic analysis research facility for the U.S. Department of Homeland Security:

* Brookhaven National Laboratory, Upton, New York
* Idaho National Laboratory, Idaho Falls, Idaho
* Lawrence Livermore National Laboratory, Livermore, California
* National Biodefense Analysis and Countermeasures Center, Frederick, Maryland
* National Renewable Energy Laboratory, Golden, Colorado
* Oak Ridge National Laboratory, Oak Ridge, Tennessee
* Pacific Northwest National Laboratory, Richland, Washington

Battelle is also part of a consortium that manages the National Nuclear Laboratory in the United Kingdom.

Battelle Ventures: This independent venture fund, financed by Battelle, helps move new technology into the marketplace by providing seed and early-stage capital to technology companies.

Education: Since its founding, Battelle has actively supported education. Today Battelle supports initiatives in Ohio and across the United States that measure student achievement, assist with professional development for teachers and promote inquiry-based learning, especially in the science, technology, engineering, and mathematics (STEM) disciplines.

For more information, visit www.battelle.com.

Opposite page: Headquarters for Battelle, the world's largest independent R&D organization in health and life sciences, national security, and energy, the environment, and material sciences.

Accentuare

Accenture is a global management consulting, technology services, and outsourcing company, with more than 215,000 people serving clients in more than 120 countries.

Combining unparalleled experience, comprehensive capabilities across all industries and business functions, and extensive research on the world's most successful companies, Accenture collaborates with clients to help them become high-performance businesses and governments. The company generated net revenues of US$21.6 billion for the fiscal year ended Aug. 31, 2010.

Accenture's high-performance business strategy builds on the company's expertise in consulting, technology, and outsourcing to help clients perform at the highest levels so they can create sustainable value for their customers and shareholders. Using industry knowledge, service-offering expertise, and technology capabilities, Accenture identifies new business and technology trends and develop solutions to help clients around the world to enter new markets; increase revenues in existing markets; improve operational performance; and deliver their products and services more effectively and efficiently.

Accenture has extensive relationships with the world's leading companies and governments and work with organizations of all sizes—including 94 of the Fortune Global 100 and more than three quarters of the Fortune Global 500. Accenture's commitment to client satisfaction strengthens and extends these relationships. For example, of the company's top 100 clients in fiscal year 2009, based on revenue, 99 have been clients for at least five years, and 91 have been clients for at least 10 years.

Company Strengths

Among the many strengths that distinguish Accenture in the marketplace are its extensive industry expertise, broad and evolving service offerings, and expertise in business transformation outsourcing. Accenture has a long history of technology innovation and implementation, including extensive research and development capabilities, on which the company spend approximately $300 million annually.

Committed to the long-term development of its employees, Accenture has created a proven and experienced management team that strives to meet and exceed the expectations of its clients.

Core Values

Accenture's core values have shaped the culture and defined the character of the company, guiding how it behaves and makes decisions. These core values, which are listed below, reflect a strong ethical framework and sense of individual responsibility that are sometimes lacking in the corporate world:

Stewardship: Building a heritage for future generations, acting with an owner mentality, developing people everywhere we are, and meeting our commitments to all internal and external stakeholders.

Best People: Attracting and developing the best talent for our business, stretching our people, and developing a "can-do" attitude.

Client Value Creation: Improving our clients' business performance, creating long-term, win-win relationships, and focusing on execution excellence.

One Global Network: Mobilizing the power of teaming to deliver consistently exceptional service to our clients anywhere in the world.

Respect for the Individual: Valuing diversity, ensuring an interesting and inclusive environment, and treating people as we would like to be treated ourselves.

Integrity: Inspiring trust by taking responsibility, acting ethically, and encouraging honest and open debate.

By enhancing consulting and outsourcing expertise with alliances and other capabilities, Accenture helps move clients forward in every part of their businesses, from strategic planning to day-to-day operations. With approximately 215,000 people serving clients in more than 120 countries, deep industry and business process expertise, broad global resources, and a proven track record, Accenture can mobilize the right people, skills, and technologies to help clients improve their performance and achieve the desired results.

Sequent

Provide services that help businesses take care of their people, Sequent offers a continuum of integrated services, from strategic consulting services to a wide variety of technology-enabled Human Resources Outsourcing Services.

Consulting Services

Through its Consulting Services, Sequent specializes in helping companies grow by developing their people and maximizing their bottom-line profits. Sequent works hard to "listen between the lines" so that it can help its clients distinguish between what they want and what they need. It all begins with a thorough understanding of an organization's needs. This is the foundation for helping clients achieve their goals. Sequent offers consulting services in Organizational Development, Talent Management, and Technology Solutions.

Human Resources Outsourcing Services

Through its Human Resources Outsourcing Services, Sequent's goal is to free up business owners to focus on what they do best—running their business. By outsourcing their human resources to Sequent, they are better able to care for their employees while they focus on their core business. Sequent has years of experience working with a wide range of businesses across many industries to help contain costs and increase productivity, reduce liability, and improve profits by attracting, retaining, and aligning talent. Essentially, Sequent provides a higher level of expertise and breadth of resources than what most small- to medium-sized businesses have in-house.

Trusted Advisors to Clients

The organizations with which Sequent works depend on the company to have their best interests in mind. Sequent's experience allows the company to help clients solve complex business issues, earning their trust as a key advisor.

Company Achievements

In 1995 William F. Hutter founded the company on the belief that he could build a better way to serve the client. Since then, Sequent has grown to offer a continuum of integrated services, from strategic consulting services to a wide variety of technology-enabled Human Resources outsourcing services. www.sequent.biz.

Above: The Sequent Solution Center, located in Dublin, Ohio. Sequent is one of the top 100 privately held businesses in central Ohio, with offices in Columbus, Ohio; Birmingham, Alabama; and Springfield, Ohio.

PROFILES OF COMPANIES AND ORGANIZATIONS
Manufacturing

Commercial Vehicle Group, Inc.

Commercial Vehicle Group, Inc. is a recognized world leader in the development, manufacture, and fulfillment of fully integrated system solutions for the commercial vehicle market.

CVG's brands include KAB Seating™, National Seating, Sprague Devices®, Prutsman, Moto Mirror®, RoadWatch®, Road Scan®, ComforTEK™, FlameTEK™, and Bostrom Seating®.

Leading CVG customers include Caterpillar, Volvo/Mack, Navistar, Daimler Trucks North America, Oshkosh, PACCAR, Deere & Company, and Komatsu. CVG also has contracts with major manufactures such as Hino (a Toyota company), XCMG and Beiqi Foton Motor Company, heavy-equipment and large-truck manufactures located in China and Skoda Auto in the Czech Republic.

CVG employs approximately 5,430 employees and has operations in Alabama, Arizona, Indiana, Illinois, Iowa, North Carolina, Ohio, Oregon, Tennessee, Virginia, and Washington. Outside the United States, CVG has operations and offices in Australia, Belgium, China, the Czech Republic, Mexico, Ukraine, and the United Kingdom.

CVG's strategy is to seek growth by increasing the company's global presence and expanding its product offerings through acquisitions, marketing activities, and research and development. Founded in 1997 as Trim Systems, the company expanded in 2000 with the acquisition of National Seating, KAB Seating, Sprague Devices, Moto Mirror, and Prutsman. In 2004 the company became publicly traded (NASDAQ: CVGI) under its then-new name, Commercial Vehicle Group, Inc. Expanding its global footprint with the opening of CVG Shanghai, the company acquired Mayflower, C.I.E.B., Cabarrus Plastics, and Monona Wire Corporation. In 2011 CVG acquired Bostrom Seating® in the United States and Stratos Seating in Australia, giving it an expanded presence in the heavy-vehicle Original Equipment Manufacturer (OEM) seating market, the commercial-vehicle aftermarket, and international military seating markets. In 2011 CVG also formed a new joint venture in India.

In 2008 the company moved into its three-story, 89,000-square-foot corporate complex in New Albany, Ohio. The facility includes a 37,500-square-foot, state-of-

CVG's vision is to be the preferred global supplier to the commercial vehicle market. To achieve that vision, the company is focused on securing assembly contracts for commercial vehicle cabs and interiors, eliminating costs and expanding its product capabilities to offer complete subsystems for heavy-truck, construction, agriculture, marine, and specialty-vehicle markets on a global basis.

This page: CVG's Corporate Headquarters and Research & Development Center in New Albany, Ohio.

CVG's products include suspension seat systems, interior trim systems (including instrument and door panels, headliners, cabinetry, molded products and floor systems), cab structures and components, mirrors, wiper systems, electronic wiring harness assemblies, and controls and switches.

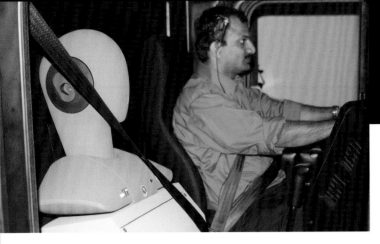

the-art Research & Development center, which is home to a cutting-edge Acoustics & Thermal Lab where skilled technicians pinpoint sources of noise and temperature loss or gain in a cab. A Multi-Axis Performance Simulator creates maximum thrust and translational stroke in a controlled laboratory setting, simulating the conditions experienced by drivers on the highway. The 6-Axis Performance Lab creates in weeks conditions that would normally take years or thousands of miles in actual service, greatly accelerating performance testing and reducing time lost in errors or rework.

The Biomechanics and Ergonomics Simulation and Test Mobile Laboratory can monitor the gaze, reaction, and muscular stress of an operator providing real-time data that is used to engineer innovative operator stations, including seats, controls and vision.

Concept Cab

Unveiled at the 63rd Internationale Automobil-Ausstellung (IAA) Commercial Vehicle Show in Hannover, Germany, CVG's innovative Concept Cab includes features such as ventilated and heated seats to optimize driver comfort and mini-mize HVAC usage. The cab also incorporates concept electric power generators driven by air flow and vehicle motion to power in-cab electrical components.

Excellence and Entrepreneurship

The recipient of numerous honors, CVG has received several major awards, including selection by John Deere for Partner Status, five Quality Q-Awards from Skoda (a part of the Volkswagen Group), and the Caterpillar SQEP for the third year in a row. CVG also received the Henry Ford Technology Award and was honored for CAT Supplier Excellence, Freightliner Masters of Quality, MAN Supplier of the Year, and Paccar Quality Achievement.

FlameTEK™, a self-extinguishing interior trim product for passenger bus, rail, aviation, marine, commercial, and military vehicle applications, was named a 2011 TechColumbus Innovation Awards Semi-Finalist. CVG's leadership garnered several other accolades, including Entrepreneur of the Year Finalist from Ernst & Young, and Business of the Year and CEO of the Year awards from the New Albany Chamber of Commerce.

Dedicated to giving back to the community, CVG supports a number of philanthropic organizations, including the Salvation Army, the New Albany Community Foundation, the Junior League of Columbus, Operation Support Our Troops, and the Columbus Food Bank. Joining in the fight to eradicate disease, CVG contributes to the Cystic Fibrosis Foundation, Nationwide Children's Hospital, and the Leukemia Society. CVG supports youth through New Albany school athletics and partnerships with OSU, Ohio University, and Otterbein University. For its philanthropic efforts, CVG received the 2010 Pillar Award for Community Service.

For more information, visit www.cvgrp.com.

This page, from left:
Research and Development
Acoustics Testing;
CVG's Global Seat.

Momentive: A Leader in Sustainability

Momentive is a leading global provider of specialty chemicals and materials, headquartered in Columbus, Ohio, with annual sales of more than $7.5 million. Over 20,000 customers around the globe use Momentive's broad range of specialty materials to improve the performance of their end products.

This page: Momentive is focused not only on the sustainability of its own products, but also on helping customers create more environmentally suitable offerings. It provides the materials that make wind turbines more cost-effective, power lines more efficient, and natural gas more accessible.

Materials from Momentive are used in a wide variety of industries, with end-use applications that touch nearly every part of modern living. Thousands of everyday objects incorporate Momentive's innovative materials, from cosmetics and medical devices to the engineered wood used to build and furnish homes, to high-voltage insulators, to smart phones and flat-screen TVs, to automobiles and planes—the list is endless.

Because its output is so substantial and widespread, Momentive is highly aware of its responsibility to society and the environment. Consequently the company is committed to being an industry leader in sustainability and sound environmental practices. At Momentive 'sustainability' means many things: reducing the environ-

mental impact of its products, operating facilities, and plants with a focus on reducing waste and being socially responsible.

Most important, at Momentive sustainability is not an afterthought. It is built into each and every aspect of the business, from the ground up.

Products that Make the World Better

First and foremost, Momentive employs the principles of green chemistry, the practice of developing and manufacturing chemicals in a manner that is sustainable, safe, and nonpolluting. When measuring environmental impact, Momentive considers each product's entire life cycle, including design, manufacture, and use. "Green" chemists on staff are constantly devising new ways to decrease consumption of materials and energy while reducing waste.

To meet green chemistry standards, Momentive scrutinizes all potential new products for sustainability. To be considered more sustainable, new products must generate savings in energy, greenhouse gas, water, or waste during production or customer use; contain increased renewable material; be more recyclable; and/or be safer.

Because the entire supply chain matters, Momentive seeks out sustainability-oriented vendors for its raw materials and minimizes the environmental impact of packaging and shipping.

Producing with an Eye on the Environment

In addition to developing greener products, Momentive strives to operate its plants and offices in a sustainable fashion. This starts with each facility recording all of

the resources it uses and waste it produces on a monthly basis and sharing the information across its network of 104 global manufacturing locations. In this way, the company can set baselines.

For instance, each operating site tracks how many metric tons of greenhouse gases (GHG) are released into the atmosphere annually, with an eye toward future reductions. GHG emitted by others on behalf of Momentive (e.g., from an electric company burning natural gas or coal) are included in this calculation.

Sustainable operation means conserving resources such as water and energy. By differentiating between virgin water, process water, storm water, and sanitary sewer water, Momentive can selectively recycle. This reuse lessens the overall volume of water used and wastewater produced. Energy Leaders, whose sole responsibility is to promote efficiency, are deployed throughout the company.

Maximizing Safety

Acting sustainably is also about maximizing safety for Momentive's people, customers, and communities. To ensure the company is always operating in an environmentally responsible manner, all employees are well-versed in Momentive's Environmental Health and Safety Policy as well as in relevant standards and procedures. Momentive facilities are certified safe and have won many leading accreditations including ISO 1400, 1401, and 1408.

Integrating Sustainability into the Business Culture

Sustainability is about more than just the environment. It means management that systematically increases consistency and efficiency across an organization. Human as well as natural resources must be used as efficiently as possible. Every employee hour spent on an unproductive task is waste, too.

Momentive incorporates Six Sigma business management strategies throughout its organization to improve business processes and reduce errors not just in manufacturing but across all facets of the business. This approach has yielded considerable savings for Momentive and its customers while making the company more efficient.

To attract, develop, and retain a world-class workforce, Momentive is continually improving the work environment through facility enhancements, while working to build a culture of customer focus, innovation, and sustainability. The company provides competitive compensation, benefits packages, and employee development programs. It also encourages employees to transplant the spirit of sustainability into their communities via numerous service and volunteerism initiatives.

By taking an integrated approach to sustainability—from reducing the environmental impact of its products to improving operational discipline in its plants to making environmental consciousness part of its corporate culture—Momentive has become a leader and innovator in making the world a greener place. For more information, visit the Web site at www.momentive.com.

This page, from left: Momentive materials are key components in airplanes and automobiles, making them lighter and more fuel-efficient; indoor air quality has improved over the past three decades thanks to advances in wood adhesive technology championed by Momentive; Momentive technology has helped reduce the volume of pesticide used in the spraying of fields.

TS Tech North America

Designing comfortable, high-quality automobile seats and interiors at a competitive price, TS Tech North America works to satisfy millions of global customers to a level "Beyond Comfort."

This page: TS Tech strives to create a culture in which associates have the opportunity to provide input and improve upon their job processes.

Established in December 1960, TS Tech Co. LTD. enjoys a worldwide reputation for the development and production of automobile interior products, including seats, door trim, and roof trim. TS Tech, which celebrated its 50th anniversary in December 2010, also develops and manufactures components for motorcycles, including seats, fenders, and more.

TS Tech's development facilities are based in the Technical Center in Tochigi Prefecture and at its U.S. subsidiary, TS Tech North America, Inc., in Reynoldsburg, Ohio. New product development and validation takes place at these sites, along with sales, purchasing, quality engineering, industrial engineering, administration, business planning, and engineering functions. To enhance overall product attractiveness to the market, TS Tech sets its own quality targets higher than those demanded by its clients, with every site and division world-wide working together to hit these targets at all stages of planning. A QCDDM (Quality, Cost, Delivery, Development, Management) structure is in place at the upstream stage prior to production, ensuring a smooth flow from development through full-scale production with no allowance for down time.

TS Tech's LPL (Large Project Leader) System supports new product development. Put in place to manage all divisions and overseas offices associated with a product development project, the LPL provides total management from planning proposals through commercial production. The LPL serves as the point of contact with the client and ensures the development of highly competitive and attractive products that are unique to TS Tech.

The development stage employs high-grade IT systems and equipment, including CAD, utilizing the full Catia V5 Suite, and CAE, utilizing LS Dyna and other products.

To develop products with proven levels of superior safety, the Safety Technical Center in Tochigi Prefecture and TS Tech North America Inc. have installed dynamic testing equipment, which simulates conditions (shock wave types) very close to those experienced during an actual vehicle collision. The vast store of experimental data generated from these tests allows the engineers to perform highly accurate collision testing and evaluations, along with CAE-based analysis.

Based on the results of safety-related research and development, TS Tech develops seating that alleviates the impact on the neck during rear-end collisions and seat weight sensor systems to control the deployment of air bags based on the body weight of the passenger. TS Tech is also developing commercial applications for occupant protection seat technology, which alleviates harm to passengers in front-end collisions.

To ensure that quality targets are met for each product, the production engineering division provides input from the earliest developmental stages, relying on production planning and production methodologies required to achieve stable product quality outcomes. TS Tech products have been earning high evaluation marks for the past several years in initial quality surveys (IQS) published by the J.D. Power and Associates, a U.S, research institute.

To help create a resource-circulating society, TS Tech is actively working toward environmentally friendly manufacturing, In addition to reducing product weight to improve vehicles' fuel efficiency, TS Tech is also developing technologies to reduce the number of components and improve product recyclability. Each division strives to minimize and properly treat waste materials and contaminants, recycle materials, and use resources and energy efficiently.

Serving the Community

As a part of its Corporate Social Responsibility initiative, TS Tech also actively serves the communities in which it operates. The company collects public donations for the victims of devastating natural disasters such as the massive earthquake and tsunami that occurred in Japan in 2011. Other activities include involvement and support of Operation Feed, Columbus Food Bank, the American Cancer Society's Relay for Life, Air National Guard—Rickenbacker Air Base (Families of Deployed soldiers), Angel Tree, Volunteers of America's Operation Backpack, and Breast Cancer Awareness Lee Denim Day. TS Tech makes donations for Christmas presents for children from financially challenged households in the Reynoldsburg area.

To ensure long-term growth in an uncertain world economy, TS Tech is focusing on the rising demand for compact vehicles in emerging countries poised for growth. The company will also pursue the development of new lightweight products that are comfortable, safe, and environmentally friendly.

For more information on TS Tech products, visit www.tstech.co.jp/english/

This page, from left:
Crash simulation testing
is used to determine TS
Tech product capabilities.
TS Tech's Reynoldsburg
campus, established in
1994, is occupied by TS
Tech North America, Inc.
and one of its central Ohio
manufacturing plants, TS
Tech USA Corporation.

Worthington Industries

In 1955 John H. McConnell purchased his first load of steel by borrowing $600 against his 1952 Oldsmobile. From these modest beginnings, McConnell started Worthington Industries, a company known for its innovative products and services as well as its unique employee relationships.

McConnell set as the foundation of the company a philosophy that is grounded in the Golden Rule and is very much a part of the company more than 55 years later. Today Worthington Industries is sustainability in motion thanks to the commitment of more than 8,500 employees in 12 countries around the world.

Worthington Industries—widely recognized as North America's premier, value-added steel processor and a leader in manufactured metal products—is comprised of three main business segments: steel processing, pressure cylinders, and metal framing. Worthington also has established a reputation as an originator of successful joint ventures. Collectively these business segments provide solutions to more than 7,000 customers in industries as diverse as:

Agriculture	HVAC
Appliance	Industrial
Automotive	Lawn and garden
Construction	Leisure and recreation
Electrical control	Medical
Energy	Office furniture
Hardware	Retail

Steel Processing

Worthington Steel is recognized as the largest business segment of Worthington Industries and is America's largest independent processor of flat-rolled steel. It provides the value-added and innovative bridge between the capabilities of major steel producers and the specialized needs of end users.

Pressure Cylinders

Worthington Cylinders is a global leader offering the most complete line of pressure cylinders in the industry including storage of liquefied petroleum, refrigerants, oxygen, industrial gases, and compressed natural gas. Employee ingenuity and the acquisition of strong brands have strengthened the product line, leveraging the company's pressure-cylinder expertise to create retail-ready products, including Coleman® camping cylinders, BernzOmatic® hand torches, Balloon Time® helium tank kits, and Worthington Pro Grade® products.

Joint Ventures

Innovative companies consistently seek out new markets and opportunities. Worthington's pursuit of joint ventures affords the company market exploration with new products while sharing in the operating risk and resources as well as the reward.

This page: Worthington offers value-added steel processing.

Photos (this page and opposite page, right): Carmon Rinehart.

Worthington has earned a loyal supplier and customer base, the confidence of shareholders, accolades from business influencers, and success admired by many. Its successful trajectory has been uncommon, especially in the volatile world of raw materials manufacturing and fabrication.

The company went public in 1968, moved to the New York Stock Exchange in 2000, and three years later was recognized as one of the 30 best-performing stocks of the past 30 years by *Money* magazine. Respected publications regularly name the company to high-profile annual lists, including Fortune, Industry Week, and Forbes. Fortune's 100 Best Companies to Work For has recognized Worthington four times since the listing began in 1997.

Doing the Right Thing

Worthington Industries' achievements to date are significant, but it's the company's commitment to continuous improvement and doing the right thing on behalf of its employees, the environment, and the communities in which it operates that has made a lasting impression. Worthington's SafeWorks program is the company's commitment to a goal of zero recordable injuries. As a result, many facilities have experienced significant stretches of time—in some cases nearly 10 years— without lost time incidents, as well as periods of more than a year without a recordable injury. Worthington's safety efforts have earned them a spot as "One of America's Safest Companies" by *EHS Today*.

Worthington upholds its commitment to environmental stewardship through programs it employs and products it offers. The company recycles 100 percent of steel scrap and ferrous oxide, which represent the company's two largest waste streams. Worthington has steadily reduced energy consumption, with marked decreases occurring every year since 2003. Further, its innovative DC FlexZone Ceilings—a Green Building Council Signature Product—is a low-voltage grid ceiling with plug-and-play flexibility that is compatible with renewable energy resources, making LED lighting, solar, wind, and fuel cell power even more efficient.

Community Engagement

Community engagement is a local matter, meaning that facilities are empowered to make decisions on how best to serve the communities in which they operate while giving employees the opportunity to impact their community. Additionally, the company operates the Worthington Industries Foundation, which gave nearly $5 million to worthy endeavors in the last five years alone.

These innovative businesses and conscientious business practices—together with visionary leadership and dedicated employees—are what comprise a vibrant and sustainable Worthington Industries.

To learn more about Worthington Industries, visit the Web site at www.worthingtonindustries.com.

This page, from left: International metal-framed construction; the company's comprehensive line of pressure cylinders serves 70-plus countries; Worthington's motivated workforce has extensive manufacturing expertise.

METTLER TOLEDO

A global manufacturer and marketer of precision instruments for use in laboratory, industrial, and food retailing applications, METTLER TOLEDO enjoys global number-one market positions in a majority of its businesses.

Above, from left: METTLER TOLEDO instruments are used in research, scientific, and quality-control labs, among many others, in pharmaceutical, chemical, food, and cosmetics industries. METTLER TOLEDO provides weighing solutions that help customers by automating processes, increasing yields, controlling product quality, and complying with industry standards and regulations.

The company has deep roots in Ohio, dating back to 1901, when Toledo Scale was founded. In 1989 Mettler Instrument AG acquired Toledo Scale Corporation, thereby linking the two global weighing leaders and forming the new company METTLER TOLEDO. A public company since 1997, METTLER TOLEDO (MTD) is listed on the NYSE.

METTLER TOLEDO's worldwide sales and service network is one of the most extensive in the industry, with more than 12,000 trained, experienced employees serving the specialized needs of a global customer base. Of the approximately 3,000 employees located within the Americas, approximately 700 are based in the central Ohio area.

Manufacturing Facilities

METTLER TOLEDO's manufacturing facilities are located in the United States, Germany, the United Kingdom, Switzerland, and China. In addition to the North American headquarters, two manufacturing facilities call Columbus, Ohio, their home. The Masstron facility is the company's global competence center for vehicle scales, floor scales, and tank-weighing modules. These products are fabricated from either carbon or stainless steel in order to support a range of applications serving a wide variety of industrial segments.

The Worthington facility focuses on engineering and developing leading solutions for retail and industrial customers. It features a state-of-the-art metrology lab, high-end assembly operations, and spare-parts fulfillment for the company's North American customers.

Products and Solutions

METTLER TOLEDO's array of products, solutions, and services is available in more than a hundred countries, helping customers to address many of their critical work challenges. Through instruments, software solutions, and service offerings, customers can streamline work processes, improve product quality, enhance throughput, and achieve regulatory compliance.

METTLER TOLEDO's vast product portfolio is supported by the experience, skills, and thorough know-how of the company's far-reaching, dedicated service specialists team. These thousands of trusted advisors span the globe, bringing local expertise to enhance the uptime, compliance, and performance of the customers' processes.

For further information on METTLER TOLEDO, visit www.mt.com.

Norse Dairy Systems (NDS)

Norse Dairy Systems provides ice cream novelty manufacturers with the highest-quality products and filling equipment for the production of frozen novelty products, from ice cream sandwiches to push-tube treats.

In 1928, with the invention of the sundae cone, Norse Dairy Systems (NDS) established itself as a leader in the ice cream novelty field. Headquartered in Columbus, Ohio, Norse developed several key novelty products and production systems that are still widely used today, including the ice cream sandwich filling machine (1945), the first automated cone filling machine (1954), and the push-tube treat (1960). NDS's comprehensive range of products include ice cream sandwich wafers, sugar cones, baked ingredients, sleeves, push-tube treats, and novelty cups, as well as state-of-the-art equipment systems to support novelty production. Even in the 21st century, NDS continues to innovate, introducing the first use of

robotics in ice cream novelty production in 2005, as well as continued updates in controls technology and packing solutions.

Servicing customers in over 20 countries, NDS is focused on quality processes to ensure customer satisfaction with all products, programs, and services. NDS maintains practices and certification in Material Resource Planning (MRP) and British Retail Consortium (BRC). An experienced engineering staff designs novelty filling systems, innovative valving, and automated packing solutions utilizing the latest in production technology. Customer service representatives address service needs and manage orders from time of placement through shipping and billing, tracking many service performance measures to ensure high levels of order compliance and customer satisfaction.

NDS offers a complete service program to ensure that customers' systems perform at peak efficiency. This service includes Training Works, a program to certify operators, maintenance engineers, and sanitarians, ensuring that customers achieve maximum efficiency from NDS equipment. Using a modular curriculum, Training Works sessions are designed for both new and experienced operators. On-site training for Basic Operation training allows employees to learn on the job. Advanced Operation and Maintenance training held at the Columbus facility provides trainees with access to the engineers, technicians, and field service engineers who designed, built, and maintain the equipment. A hotline provides immediate answers to questions, and experienced field service engineers are on call to provide any needed adjustments or repairs.

NDS continues to explore new possibilities for frozen novelties. By closely monitoring emerging trends in customers' markets around the country and globally, NDS helps its customers identify areas of opportunity in their product portfolios and to conceptualize new products. For more information, visit the Web site at www.norse.com.

Norse Dairy Systems is headquartered in Columbus, Ohio.

PROFILES OF COMPANIES AND ORGANIZATIONS
Nutrition

Abbott Nutrition

For nearly 125 years, Abbott has been a worldwide leader in nutrition science, research, and development, and its people have been driven by a constant goal: to advance medical science to help people live healthier lives.

Columbus-based Abbott Nutrition is part of Abbott, a global, broad-based health care company devoted to the discovery, development, manufacturing, and marketing of pharmaceuticals and medical products, including nutritionals, devices, and diagnostics. The company employs nearly 90,000 people and markets its products in more than 130 countries.

Behind every Abbott product—from market-leading medicines, to advanced medical devices, to trusted infant formulas and adult nutritional products—is a desire to make a difference in the lives of the patients, consumers, caregivers, and health care professionals that Abbott serves.

Abbott's nutrition products have been household names in Columbus and across the nation for more than 100 years. The Moores & Ross Milk Company was founded in Columbus, Ohio, in 1903 as a partnership between Harry C. Moores and Stanley M. Ross. Facilities consisted of a rented storeroom at 429 East Long Street, near the downtown area of Columbus, where fresh milk was processed and bottled for home delivery.

The business prospered and, in 1924, the partners took the daring move to produce and market a then-new concept: milk-based infant formula. The new venture proved so successful that, by 1928, the company had changed its name to M&R Dietetic Laboratories and sold its dairy operations to another prominent Columbus firm, the Borden Company. Now free to concentrate fully on the emerging field of pediatric nutrition, M&R Dietetic Laboratories created one of the most respected and successful infant formula products—Similac.

This page, from left: What began in 1903 as the Moores & Ross Milk Company continues today as Abbott Nutrition, which has set the standard for science-based nutrition and innovative nutritional products and solutions to support the growth, health, and wellness for people around the world. In 1925 Moores and Ross took the daring step of producing and marketing milk-based infant formula, known as Franklin Infant Food. Today Abbott's infant formula product line is known worldwide as Similac.

In 1964 the company—by then renamed Ross Products Division—was acquired by North Chicago-based Abbott, a world leader in health care products. In 2007 Ross changed its name to Abbott Nutrition.

Today Abbott is a worldwide leader in nutrition science, research, and development. Hundreds of experienced scientists collaborate daily to translate leading-edge research into a wide range of science-based infant formulas, nutrition products for toddlers and children, medical nutritionals, nutrition and energy bars, and related products to support the growth, health, and wellness of people of all ages.

Nutrition Solutions for People of All Ages

With its North American headquarters in Columbus, where it employs more than 2,000 employees, Abbott Nutrition has additional U.S. manufacturing locations in Arizona, Michigan, Virginia, and California, as well as outside the U.S. in China, Singapore, Ireland, The Netherlands, and Spain. Abbott's experienced scientists collaborate every day in state-of-the-art laboratories to develop cutting-edge nutrition products and conduct clinical studies in human nutrition.

Abbott is a respected leader in helping babies grow and develop. Similac, the first iron-fortified infant formula in the United States to help prevent iron-deficiency anemia, was launched in the early 20th century. Today the Similac product line includes hypoallergenic, soy, organic, sensitive formulas—and more specialty infant products—to help moms nourish babies no matter what their nutritional needs.

Abbott holds to a high standard when it comes to infant nutrition. Similac formulas have been developed with leading scientists through more than 280 clinical studies. The company also develops and markets nutritional formulas to help parents manage feeding problems such as fussiness, gas, and diarrhea, as well as specialized products for premature infants, and infants and children with food allergies or metabolic illnesses.

Abbott also offers a broad selection of adult nutritional products. These include Ensure®, leading adult nutritional drinks that are a source of Complete, Balanced Nutrition®; EAS® bars, shakes, and supplements for athletic consumers with fitness goals; and ZonePerfect®, nutritious snacks for consumers on the go.

Besides well-known consumer brands, Abbott provides a wide range of medical foods and related products to meet the distinct dietary needs of people with serious health conditions such as diabetes, cancer, and respiratory disorders. Glucerna® was the first therapeutic nutritional product for people with diabetes. And the company's specialized nutrition products, such as EleCare®, aid infants and children with multiple food allergies, severe gastrointestinal impairment, and metabolic diseases.

This page: Abbott continues to advance the science of nutrition through world-class research and development.

top 10 "Best Companies for Working Mothers" for 10 straight years by *Working Mother* magazine and one of the "Top 50 Companies for Diversity" by *Diversity Inc.* magazine for the past six years. Abbott has also been recognized as a top employer of scientists, and a top employer in multiple countries around the world.

Citizenship

Abbott views its commitment to global citizenship as another opportunity to improve lives around the world. In 2010 Abbott and the Abbott Fund invested approximately $600 million in grants, patient assistance programs, humanitarian support, product donations, and community programs, reaching millions of people around the world.

This page: Abbott's broad range of nutritional products, state-of-the-art manufacturing facilities and processes, and dedication to quality and safety have earned worldwide consumer trust.

Workplace Excellence

Abbott recognizes that all of its employees are essential to the company's continued success. The company focuses on attracting and retaining the best and brightest talent through opportunities such as comprehensive development programs, formal career growth plans, and international assignments, among others. A longstanding commitment to its employees has earned Abbott recognition as one of the

This commitment includes the Columbus community, where Abbott Nutrition works to advance nutrition and nutrition education. It sponsors and supports programs each year, providing hands-on science programs to children, thousands of dollars and volunteer hours to the Mid Ohio Food Bank, and educational science programs to students and visitors to Center of Science and Industry (COSI), as well as involvement with several other community partners.

Abbott was a recipient of the 2011 Columbus Business First Corporate Caring Award, in recognition of its corporate philanthropy and community outreach. In 2009 Abbott Nutrition received a LifeCare Alliance Project OpenHand Corporate Leadership Spirit award for outstanding commitment in furthering the mission of Project OpenHand, a nonprofit organization that supplies meals and food bank services for HIV/AIDS survivors. Additionally, Abbott Nutrition received the Central Ohio March of Dimes 2008 Lifetime Achievement Award, which recognizes individuals and organizations who have demonstrated exemplary leadership in maternal and infant health.

Other awards include Prevent Blindness Ohio's 2005 "People of Vision" Award that recognizes Ohio companies and their top leadership for outstanding involvement in the community, and the "National Kashrut (Kosher) Award" for more than 40 years of trusted service with the Orthodox Union (OU), the nation's largest kosher certification agency.

Poised for Growth

Abbott is poised to continue to grow through its diverse line of products and innovative, highly effective solutions that are helping people around the world pursue healthier lives. Helping to drive that growth will be the hundreds of Abbott Nutrition employees in Columbus and the thousands more across the nation and around the world who are committed to excellence and share a desire to make a difference in the lives of patients, consumers, caregivers, and health care professionals.

For more information, visit www.abbottnutrition.com.

This page: Abbott works with local community organizations, such as the Columbus Mid-Ohio Food Bank, where employee volunteerism also makes a difference.

PROFILES OF COMPANIES AND ORGANIZATIONS
Professional Services

The Charles Penzone Salons

Offering a full range of services by skilled professionals, The Charles Penzone Salons are on the cutting edge of the beauty industry.

This page,
clockwise from left:
The lobby of The Grand
Salon at Polaris Parkway
includes a retail area and
complimentary beverage bar;
hair stations at MAX The
Salon in Short North;
Charles and Debra Penzone.

In the 1970s, a young entrepreneur had a dream—to become a leader in the beauty industry. Starting with a $500 loan and three employees, Charles Penzone opened a 600-square-foot hair salon in Upper Arlington, outside Columbus. He continued to grow the company over the next 20 years, and by 1989, he had expanded to six salons with more than 150 employees.

Penzone's vision of a full-service, free-standing salon and day spa became a reality in 1991 with the consolidation of six salons and the introduction of the first Grand Salon in Dublin, Ohio. The 18,000-square-foot facility provided three floors of hair styling and manicure stations, massage and skin care rooms, a training room, and a tranquil private garden. Two years later, the Grand Salon in Dublin was named Salon of the Year by *Modern Salon* magazine. The revolutionary Grand Salon concept was featured on *The Today Show* and *Inside Edition* and in *People* magazine, *In Style* magazine and *Redbook*. In 1993 his wife Debra, herself a hair care professional, assumed a leadership role, becoming Training Director/Creative Director.

In 1996 the remaining salons were consolidated into the 20,000-square-foot Grand Salon in Gahanna/New Albany—at the time the world's largest, most luxurious salon and day spa. During its second year, the new facility received *Modern Salon Magazine*'s Salon of the Year Award. The Grand Salon at Polaris Parkway, which opened in 2002, was named Salon of the Year by *Modern Salon Magazine* in 2003, a major industry honor.

MAX The Salon, a 1,100-square-foot hair salon, was introduced in 1996, providing trendy hair styles for Columbus's style-conscious clientele in upscale German Village. A second MAX The Salon opened in the trendy Short North District of downtown Columbus in 2005. Q Salon, an intimate, warehouse-themed salon, opened in 2001 in the Upper Arlington area.

The Charles Penzone Salons' full-service locations offer the following services:
• hair cut and color services
• texture and conditioning services
• manicures and pedicures
• skin care services, including facial and makeup applications
• hair removal and permanent cosmetics
• massage and hydrotherapy services

With specialty spa packages, guests can experience the tranquil relaxation room and dining room for a complete day of pampering. On- and offsite bridal services are provided to accommodate every need.

As vice president of training, Debra Penzone made major improvements to The Charles Penzone Salons Career Advancement Program (CAP) in 2005, placing a renewed focus on advanced education and training. The Charles Penzone Salons require more than 70 hours of advanced education annually for its more than 500 salon and spa professionals. Each hair and spa professional is required to fulfill 12 CP (Charles Penzone) Credits per year above and beyond state board requirements. The Professional Development Team brings in top-name hair care professionals from around the country to impart the latest nationwide trends and techniques to the team.

An innovator that continuously adapts to emerging trends, The Charles Penzone Salons launched "Curly Girl" services and DevaCurl products for Columbus' curly girls. In 2010 the salons were the first in the United States to introduce Igora Color10, a revolutionary 10-minute permanent coloration system.

In recognition of their innovative approach to the hair salon, *Salon Today* magazine named Charles and Debra Penzone as one of the Top 20 Salon Owners in 2003, and recognized them as "Power Players" in the salon and spa industry in 2008.

In 2008 an unprecedented 3,000 salon owners were nominated from 23 countries for the prestigious Global Salon Business Award for entrepreneurial spirit, and Charles Penzone was recognized as Salon Entrepreneur of the Year. In 2010 The Charles Penzone Salons were among the five finalists for the 2010 North American Hairstyling Awards (NAHA) Salon MBA Award, honoring business-savvy salon owners who have cultivated cutting-edge salons.

Giving Back to the Community

Supporting causes that empower women and assist children, The Charles Penzone Salons have been involved with Columbus's "Look Good...Feel Better" program for 13 years. Each month three salons host a two-hour program to provide women undergoing chemotherapy or radiation treatment with techniques to enhance their appearance. Debra Penzone volunteers as an Area Trainer, providing cosmetologists from other salons with the necessary tools to conduct this program. The Charles Penzone Salons are also a Gold Sponsor for Susan G. Komen Columbus Race for the Cure. For its numerous philanthropic contributions, the company was the recipient of the 2010 Pillar Award given by Smart Business Columbus. The Charles Penzone Salons are also the official hair and makeup sponsor of Fashion Week Columbus and the hair and makeup stylist for Capital Style.

Charles Penzone serves as chairman and Debra Penzone has served as president since 2008. For more information, visit www.charlespenzone.com.

This page, from left: Lobby of MAX The Salon in Short North; the lobby of The Grand Salon in Dublin; the exterior of The Grand Salon at Polaris Parkway.

Chemical Abstracts Service (CAS)

Cleaner energy, more effective medicines, safer products, and smarter solutions begin with innovation. Innovation starts with Chemical Abstracts Service (CAS).

A division of the American Chemical Society

Chemistry is the central science. As many as 30 percent of all new patents are for chemical substances, including important new pharmaceutical products. CAS is the world's authority on the chemical substances that have been publicly disclosed in journals, patents, and other reputable sources. In fact, the famous CAS "Registry" collection has reached more than 64 million specific chemical molecules, along with their structures and other important information vital to scientific research. The CAS REGISTRY^{SM} database is what patent offices turn to when deciding whether a chemical is really newly discovered.

Every day hundreds of scientists on the CAS 50-acre Columbus campus and around the globe work to build and maintain REGISTRY and other valuable CAS databases of chemical and related scientific information. New information enters CAS collections around the clock, with more than 12,000 substances being added to REGISTRY each day. CAS technology specialists also build advanced retrieval and analysis tools that enable scientists to explore the extensive CAS content easily.

This page: Columbus-based CAS has grown into a global information provider committed to serving those on the front lines of scientific discovery—researchers.

CAS: Global Leader, Local Citizen

Columbus locals may know Chemical Abstracts Service (CAS) as the home of "Picnic with the Pops" since 1983, and, most recently, as the starting point for the Pelotonia bike tour. CAS is indeed proud of its civic contributions. But scientists around the world know it as the global leader in chemical information.

Who are CAS customers? CAS serves chemical and pharmaceutical companies, universities, government organizations, and patent offices around the world. Wherever access to sophisticated information on chemical substances is required, CAS information is the choice.

CAS also fosters ingenuity at home in Columbus. As a founding member of TechColumbus, CAS works alongside Battelle, OCLC, The Ohio State University, and other local technology leaders to support programs that accelerate the growth of the city's tech-based economy.

CAS has a particularly strong historical relationship with The Ohio State University, and most recently with the James Cancer Hospital. More than 250 of the 1,400 staff working on CAS Columbus campus hold degrees from OSU, and CAS databases are a starting point for researchers seeking cures for cancer and other diseases.

Whether pursuing innovative products such as biodegradable plastics or stronger coatings for vehicles, exploring the farthest reaches of nanotechnology, or conducting prior art searches for new molecules, scientists around the world look to CAS as the database of record for molecular sciences.

CAS is the global leader in chemical information and a proud citizen of Columbus, Ohio. For more information, visit the Web site at www.cas.org.

This page, from left: More than 1,400 Ph.D. scientists, IT professionals, and other staff at CAS work continuously to develop innovative solutions for advancing global research.
Just as the CAS grounds serve as the starting line for Pelotonia, CAS databases are the place researchers begin their journey to uncover cures for cancer and other diseases.

DesignGroup

Celebrating 40 years of design, DesignGroup has altered the architectural landscape of Columbus and beyond. From the Ohio Stadium renovation to the new Franklin County Courthouse. DesignGroup has emerged as a leader in planning-based design, providing exemplary service to clients.

This page, from left: State Teachers Retirement System of Ohio; School Employees Retirement System of Ohio; The Ohio State University, Ohio Stadium.

DesignGroup was founded in 1972—as Gosnell/Essinger/Rettstatt/Weithman—by four architects with a vision and a business plan for a professional practice. The firm's name was changed to DesignGroup, Inc. in 1979 and shortened to today's DesignGroup in 2000. Since the firm's founding, DesignGroup professionals have integrated planning, architectural design, interior design, and graphic design to provide exemplary service to clients. Today the integration of these disciplines, along with the firm's focus on sustainable architecture and the use of Building Information Modeling (BIM) and other cutting-edge design tools, has helped DesignGroup become a local and regional leader in planning-based design.

The firm's practice encompasses five markets, including health care, education, libraries, civic, and workplace. DesignGroup professionals exemplify deep-seated beliefs in healthy communities, civic responsibility, life-long learning, sustainable architecture, and design that elevates.

DesignGroup's projects are part of the landscape across Columbus, the region, and beyond. The firm's work stretches as far west as Wyoming, south to Florida, north to Michigan, and east to Pennsylvania. Notable projects in the greater Columbus area include the AIA award-winning Grange Insurance Audubon Center; Columbus Metropolitan Library Main Library expansion and many of the system's branches; several buildings on The Ohio State University campus, including the Richard M. Ross Heart Hospital; the Ohio Stadium renovation; and the Martha Morehouse

Medical Plaza (formerly the J. Leonard Camera Center). Health care systems such as OhioHealth and Mt. Carmel in Columbus, along with a multitude of regional and community hospitals and health systems, have all been impacted by the firm's designs. Institutions of higher education such as Columbus College of Art & Design and Franklin University owe parts of their campuses to DesignGroup. And the skyline of downtown Columbus looks as it does because of DesignGroup's State Teachers Retirement System and School Employees Retirement System office buildings as well as the new Franklin County Courthouse.

As DesignGroup looks back in celebration on its first 40 years, it also looks ahead with great anticipation to the future of the profession and the many opportunities that will present themselves to contribute to the betterment of the built environment in Columbus and beyond. For more information, visit www.designgroup.us.com.

This page, counterclock-wise from top left: Grange Insurance Audubon Center; Goodwill Columbus; 515 E. Main Office Building; The Ohio State University Medical Center, Martha Morehouse Medical Plaza (formerly known as J. Leonard Camera Center); Franklin County Courthouse; The Ohio State University Medical Center, Richard M. Ross Heart Hospital.

Porter Wright

Commitment. Whether it's clients, the community, the profession, or the environment, Porter Wright has a long-standing tradition of meaningful commitment. Founded in 1846, the Firm has six offices located in Ohio, Florida and Washington, D.C. Its attorneys bring together knowledge, skills, and experience to represent a worldwide client base in complex legal problems and business opportunities.

Above, from left: Porter Wright attorneys work as a team to provide the best possible outcome for their clients; Porter Wright's sustainability initiative logo.

Porter Wright
Goes Green

Reduce   Reuse   Recycle

Industry publications and independent surveys such as Chambers USA, *US News & World Report*'s Best Lawyers, and the BTI Client Satisfaction Survey consistently rank Porter Wright as a national leader among legal firms. Porter Wright attorneys working across 31 practice areas and all six of the Firm's offices have been named to the *The Best Lawyers in America,* a respected peer-review publication within the legal profession.

Porter Wright attorneys focus on industry developments, changes in technology, legislative issues, and regulatory rulings that affect clients' day-to-day operations, allowing clients to remain focused on their goals. They have also set a standard of leadership in national, state, and local bar associations, judicial societies, and professional organizations. The Firm's distinguished legal staff includes 18 presidents

and past presidents of bar associations, 18 former judicial law clerks, and 7 fellows of the American College of Trial Lawyers.

By committing time and collaborating with others in the profession, the Firm expands opportunities for aspiring lawyers and ensures that meaningful legal educational programs are available. To demonstrate the Firm's commitment to diversity, the Porter Wright Morris & Arthur LLP/Ralph K. Frasier Scholarship was established in 2005 to facilitate the recruitment of minority attorneys. The scholarship consists of a cash award and a summer clerkship with the Firm. Porter Wright also helps to make legal counsel accessible to those in need, contributing thousands of hours of pro bono representation each year.

Porter Wright was an early partner in the American Bar Association's Law Office Climate Challenge program, and a pilot firm in the ABA's development of a model sustainability policy for law firms. Porter Wright's policy, modeled after the ABA policy, was adapted in 2009 and is proudly featured on the Firm's website. Porter Wright has made significant strides in recycling and reducing waste and energy use. In 2010 the Firm received the Mayor's "GreenSpotLight" Award, recognizing the steps the Firm has taken to benefit the environment.

From supporting pioneering cancer research, to providing legal services to those in need, to strengthening children's educational opportunities, to assisting families or individuals in need, to preserving local heritage, Porter Wright is committed to enriching each of its communities. Each year lawyers and staff take active roles as trustees, officers, and members of civic, charitable, and cultural organizations and dedicate their time, effort, and financial support to building stronger communities.

Porter Wright is committed to the future. The Firm enjoyed success over its first 160 years by anticipating and reacting to changes in the law, in clients' industries and businesses, and in their objectives and needs. The next 160 years promise to be even more challenging and rewarding, with strong leadership, timely legal counsel, high ethical standards, and tradition of community service continuing to guide the Firm's philosophy. For more information, visit the Firm's website at www.porterwright.com.

Above, from left: Kathleen Trafford, past president of the Columbus Bar Association, presents John Hartranft with The Bar Service Medal award at the 2009 Annual Meeting; team members of the Porter Wright Peloton begin the Pelotonia 2010.

United Retirement Plan Consultants

Since its inception in 2004, this nationally recognized retirement services company has quickly emerged as a leading national provider of retirement plan design, consulting, administration, and pension actuarial services for small and medium-sized businesses in the United States.

United
Retirement Plan
Consultants

National network. Local experts.

Above: United
Retirement Plan
Consultants'
headquarters in
Columbus, Ohio.

About United Retirement Plan Consultants

United Retirement Plan Consultants is a privately held, national firm, with headquarters in Dublin, Ohio. The firm currently operates 18 regional locations in 15 states, and services approximately 10,000 retirement plans with more than $11 billion of assets through its local operations. Through its custom acquisition and integration model, United Retirement Plan Consultants has built the industry's premier retirement services firm—offering its clients custom retirement plan design, consulting, and administration services at the regional and local level, while supported by a national network of 340 associates and the strength, stability, and efficiency of a national technology and operations backbone.

Changing the Conversation

In a seemingly crowded marketplace, each of United Retirement's more than 340 retirement plan professionals, including enrolled actuaries, accountants, attorneys, and consultants, is dedicated to the purpose of changing the typical conversation that surrounds the design and operation of a retirement plan. Quick, simple, low-cost solutions that are pre-packaged and mass-marketed to employers often miss the mark. United Retirement Plan Consultants recognized years ago that for most small and medium-sized employers, a comprehensive savings and retirement strategy involves much more than the implementation of a basic 401(k) plan. The company's President and CEO, John Davis, has set the course for delivering on that insight.

Partnering to Serve Americans' Retirement Plans

One of the core realities supporting United Retirement's strategic focus is that the retirement plan industry is experiencing change of an unprecedented scope and pace. As legislative and regulatory complexity continues to increase, aimed at enhancing and protecting the retirement savings of Americans, the demands on retirement service professionals continue to rise. As such, the retirement service industry has shifted to a specialist model, requiring service providers to alter their roles in the client-service equation from transaction-focused to consultant-based and collaborate with each other in order to deliver top-quality retirement plan strategies for their clients. United Retirement teams up with financial advisors, accountants, attorneys, record-keepers, and other industry service providers to navigate complex rules and regulations, and develop customized solutions that address each client's full range of retirement and business objectives.

A Bright Future

The company's future expansion plans are based on the strategy that has driven its growth through today: identifying and acquiring premier retirement plan consulting firms and expert professionals in key geographic markets in the U.S.; executing its proprietary platform integration strategy; and delivering on its brand promise to offer innovative, tax-efficient, and cost-effective retirement plan solutions to its clients through its growing network of associates. National Network. Local Experts.™

PROFILES OF COMPANIES AND ORGANIZATIONS
Retail/Tourism/Restaurants

Abercrombie & Fitch

Founded by David T. Abercrombie in 1892, Abercrombie & Fitch has long been known for its quality goods and premium craftsmanship. Collectively, Abercrombie & Fitch, abercrombie kids, Hollister Co., and Gilly Hicks operate retail stores in the United States, Canada, the United Kingdom, Europe, and Asia, as well as direct-to-consumer e-commerce Web sites.

As a result of a company-wide diversity initiative and recruiting strategy, A&F's demographics among in-store models and managers-in-training are now more racially and ethnically diverse than the U.S. population, the federal government, and other leading clothing retailers as a whole.

To ensure continued progress in creating a more diverse and inclusive culture, A&F relies on an Executive Diversity Council (EDC), made up of senior leaders from several business units across the organization. As an extension of the EDC, a number of associates from the Home Office, the Distribution Center, and Stores serve on Diversity Councils charged with implementing the strategies and initiatives developed by the EDC company-wide.

Philanthropy

Abercrombie & Fitch and its associates believe in supporting the communities where they do business, and are committed to being an exemplary philanthropic citizen by giving back and making a positive impact in their communities. A&F's commitment is shown through monetary and product donations, as well as countless hours of volunteer work that its associates give to a host of great causes. A&F is focused on giving back to its headquarters' local community in Columbus, Ohio, as well as nationally through nonprofit organizations. As the company continues to expand internationally, it is furthering its efforts to have a global impact, with A&F's international locations standing ready to lend support.

The Abercrombie & Fitch Home Office, in New Albany, Ohio, is home to cutting-edge facilities, technology, and resources that enable talented designers to track emerging trends and collaborate with dynamic merchandising teams to create quality products. The campus also contains more than a million square feet of distribution facilities. The close proximity of the distribution facilities to the Home Office ensures that only the highest-quality garments reach customers.

Diversity & Inclusion

Abercrombie & Fitch's corporate definition of diversity embodies all that is seen as well as what is unseen. Supporting diversity and encouraging a culture of inclusion allows A&F to better understand its customers, operate more efficiently, capitalize on the talents of its workforce, and represent the communities where it does business.

CENTRAL OHIO MEDICAL COMMUNITY Abercrombie & Fitch is proud of donations to two nationally renowned hospitals located in Columbus, Ohio. The gift to Nationwide Children's Hospital will help fund a new emergency room and trauma center for one of the busiest pediatric emergency rooms in the United States. A&F has made a commitment to donate $10 million. The gift to The Ohio State University Hospital/

Abercrombie & Fitch's campus is located on 460 acres of green space in New Albany, Ohio.

The Arthur G. James Cancer Hospital of The Ohio State University will support research and patient care initiatives in digestive diseases and women's oncology. A&F has made a commitment to raise and donate $10 million.

INTERNATIONAL RELIEF EFFORTS The Japanese earthquake and tsunami in March 2011 affected millions of people and impacted many of A&F's associates and their families directly. A&F set up an initial relief fund, and its associates around the world held their own fundraisers. Initial relief efforts provided assistance to A&F associates and their families who had been impacted by the disaster. A&F also worked with the local communities to aid in rebuilding of schools and services.

THE A&F CHALLENGE Hosted by Abercrombie & Fitch on its corporate campus, the A&F Challenge raises money to benefit various organizations and charities in central Ohio and communities in which A&F operates throughout the U.S. The A&F Challenge has raised more than $9.5 million to date.

ANNUAL FUNDRAISER/HOLIDAY CHARITY DRIVES A&F's Stores organization hosts an annual fundraising event, and employees help raise money through creative fundraising events such as skating parties, variety shows, and donating proceeds from recycling bottles. The annual fundraising and charity events have raised over $100,000 for associates in need.

During the Christmas season, the Home Office collects toys to donate to Franklin County Children Services' Child's Holiday Wish program. The Franklin County Children Services' program brings toys to over 4,500 abused, neglected, and troubled kids who otherwise wouldn't have any gifts.

Sustainability

Recognizing the importance of environmental stewardship, A&F is committed to understanding the constantly evolving impact that their business and operations have on the communities where they make and sell their products. The common goal throughout the company is to reduce waste through conservation, collaboration, and carbon emissions programs.

To focus and provide guidance for its environmental stewardship activities, A&F has adopted the Three R's concept—Reduce, Reuse, and Recycle. In 2011 Abercrombie & Fitch was awarded the Solid Waste Authority of Central Ohio (SWACO) Emerald Award in the large business category, in recognition of its sustainable efforts.

For more information, visit www.Abercrombie.com and www.anfcares.org.

A&F's wooded campus is surrounded by natural wetlands and is home to a large number of wildlife native to the area.

Big Lots

Whether it's the enticing mix of brand-name merchandise, the incomparable values, or simply the thrill of the hunt, millions of shoppers have forsaken traditional retail venues to shop at Big Lots stores for high-quality housewares, furniture, electronics, toys, and other consumer products.

have nearly nine million square feet of space and use highly automated systems to receive, prepare, load, and ship merchandise to 1,400 stores in 48 states.

Big Lots started out as Consolidated International, Inc., founded in 1967 by Sol Shenk, a visionary in the discount retail marketplace. In 1982 Consolidated Stores Corporation launched the Odd Lots closeout retail chain, with the first store located in Columbus, Ohio. With the purchase of KB Toys in 1996, Consolidated Stores doubled its size and sales. In 2001 Consolidated changed its name to Big Lots, Inc. and began converting all its stores to a single national brand. Two years later, Big Lots opened 86 new stores, remodeled 211 existing stores, expanded 242 furniture departments, and added 157 furniture departments to new and existing stores. A new $45 million national television advertising campaign provided national exposure for Big Lots. With the opening of 17 new stores in 2010, Big Lots surpassed the 1,400-

Above: Big Lots opened 17 new stores in 2010. Right: The shopping carts await the customers at this Big Lots store.

The nation's largest broadline closeout retailer, with annual revenues approaching $5 billion, Big Lots has rewritten the rules for the retail industry. Much of its success is owing to its ability to find and negotiate the best deals in brand-name closeouts from 3,000 manufacturers. Big Lots also uses its considerable buying power to purchase overstocks, package changes, buy-backs, store closings, discontinued product, excess/obsolete/distressed inventory, manufacturers' overruns, and cancelled orders.

Big Lots' distribution system is designed to ship goods quickly and efficiently to its retail outlets. Five major distribution centers, including the one in Columbus, Ohio,

store threshold with operations in all of the 48 contiguous states. In January 2011 Big Lots had the highest earnings yield in the general merchandise store industry with 8.8%, ahead of 99 Cent Stores and Target.

Big Lots has spent nearly five decades building relationships with some of the world's best-known manufacturers, With an open-to-buy exceeding $2 billion and the ability to make fast purchasing decisions, Big Lots has become the preferred solution for many big-name vendors who need to reduce their inventories. Big Lots continues to strengthen its vendor relationships by attending trade shows, meeting in person, and finding myriad ways to improve business relationships.

Big Lots Wholesale, a division of Big Lots Stores, Inc., is a business-to-business exchange providing top-quality merchandise at below-wholesale prices. Most of the merchandise sold through this division is available only to wholesale customers.

Providing timely capital solutions to consumer product companies during growth, restructuring, and change, Big Lots Capital focuses on strategic buying initiatives for Big Lots Inc. With more than 120 field staff members who can react quickly to protect assets and help with extraction, Big Lots offers fast buying decisions, prompt possession and payments, and flexible inventory distribution.

Strong leadership has helped Big Lots to weather the recent financial storm. In 2009 Big Lots CEO Steven S. Fishman was named Ernst & Young's prestigious Entrepreneur of the Year award in the business turnaround category for the South Central Ohio and Kentucky region. Since joining Big Lots in 2005, Fishman led the company through a successful WIN strategy for improving operating performance "The real honor goes to the Big Lots team for their determination and great spirit," said Fishman.

Big Lots' Big Heart

Big Lots gives back to the community through a number of programs. Big Lots and its many vendors have donated furniture, household items, and millions of dollars to efforts such as Furniture Bank's program for turning empty houses into homes for thousands of Columbus families in need. Since 1994 Big Lots has been a loyal corporate sponsor of Toys for Tots, conducting toy drives at more than 1,400 stores in 48 states. Special discounted pricing on new toys to the Toys for Tots Foundation is provided through Big Lots' Granted Wishes Program. Big Lots' Lots2Give program helps schools in need across the United States. In 2010 46 schools shared $100,000 in cash prizes from the Lots2Give video contest, with participating schools receiving 100 percent of in-store donations.

Whether contributing to worthy causes or tracking down the latest bargains for its customers, Big Lots has rightly earned its place among today's retail giants.

For more information, go to www.biglots.com.

From left. Big Lot stores offer big savings on popular consumer products. Big Lot stores feature wide aisles and attractively displayed merchandise.

Greater Columbus Convention Center

The Greater Columbus Convention Center opened in 1993 and is now one of the busiest convention facilities in North America. More than 2.5 million guests annually visit the popular complex, a perennial winner of industry accolades, including the *Facilities & Destinations* Prime Site Award and the *Association Meetings* Inner Circle Award.

in 2010 included the debut of the crown jewel of the center, Battelle Grand, which at 74,000 square feet is the largest multipurpose ballroom in Ohio. Battelle Grand was described by *The Columbus Dispatch* as "the new place to be" before it even opened, with its upscale amenities, floor-to-ceiling windows, and stunning LED ceiling lighting system capable of projecting a multitude of color combinations selected by each client.

Known as the annual home of the Arnold Sports Festival and OFA Short Course horticultural Top 200 trade show, along with hundreds of banquets, trade shows, athletic competitions, and meetings each year, the Greater Columbus Convention Center offers 410,000 square feet of exhibit space, three ballrooms, 65 meeting rooms, on-site parking, an array of service providers, and the Food Court & Shops.

Vibrant Location

The convention center is located in the midst of the vibrant Columbus High Five entertainment district and near the Arena and the Short North Arts Districts. It is also the home of the fully restored Emerson Burkhart mural *Music* and a historical marker commemorating the site of Tod Barracks and Ohio's contributions to the Civil War.

The convention center's staff participates in a variety of ongoing community endeavors, including volunteering at Cedarwood Alternative Elementary School and assisting exclusive caterer ARAMARK in preparing meals for charitable donation.

For more information on the convention center's facilities and services, visit www.columbusconventions.com.

This page: The Greater Columbus Convention Center is one of the busiest convention facilities in North America. Opposite page: Battelle Grand is the largest multipurpose ballroom in Ohio.

Managed by SMG, the world leader in venue management, marketing, and development, the venue is owned and developed by the Franklin County Convention Facilities Authority (FCCFA). The facility features a striking design by renowned architect Peter Eisenman blended with flexible meeting and exhibition space attractive to event planners. In the design process, Eisenman was inspired by the city's prominence with fiber-optic cables in the Information Age, as well as the nearby railroad tracks and highways from the site's former home, the Union Station train station.

Through continual reinvestment by the FCCFA, an expansion in 2001 increased the size of the facility to 1.7 million square feet. The $40 million renovation completed

Photo right: © D. G. Olshavsky; Left: © Ellen Dallager/Dallager Photography

White Castle

"White" signifies purity. "Castle" signifies strength, stability, and permanence. These are the qualities of the White Castle hamburger chain, which has satisfied its customers' cravings for nearly a century.

"Saturday night and it's gettin' late/

I'm gettin' hungry, I just can't wait/

Not just any kind of burger will do/

I'm being hit by those/

White Castle blues…"

—The Smithereens

This page, from left: "Three Ladies" at White Castle, ca. 1930s; White Castle #10, Wichita, ca. 1930s; customers at White Castle in New York, ca. 1947. Opposite page: White Castle #7 opened in Chicago, Sept. 22, 1929.

The foodies who chow down on sliders at gourmet restaurants owe a culinary debt to E. W. "Billy" Ingram. He opened the first White Castle in 1921 in Wichita, Kansas, selling his sliders for five cents a piece. Headquartered in Columbus since 1934, White Castle was the first hamburger chain to sell a million hamburgers and a billion hamburgers, and the first to sell frozen fast food.

Today the Smithereens and other White Castle devotees can satisfy their cravings at more than 400 locations across the Northeast and Midwest, including Chicago, Cincinnati, Cleveland, Columbus, Detroit, Indianapolis, Louisville, Minneapolis-St. Paul, Nashville, New Jersey, New York City, and St. Louis. Regional variations on the Original Slider include Düsseldorf brown mustard (Chicago, Cincinnati-Dayton, Louisville, and Nashville predominantly) and horseradish mustard (Indianapolis and St. Louis); ketchup is included automatically in New York and New Jersey, unless the customer requests otherwise.

The co-founder's grandson, E.W. "Bill" Ingram III, has served as CEO of the burger chain for 32 years. Three more third-generation and 9 fourth-generation descendants are also on board. "We really feel it's a family business in every sense of the word," said Jamie Richardson, a White Castle vice president. "It's embedded into the culture."

White Castle introduced "green" food packaging in all locations. The white paper sack and white corrugated Crave Cases have been replaced by corrugated brown paper made from 100% recycled material. "White Castle has been a responsible steward of the environment for many years in several different aspects of our businesses and operations," said Marketing Vice President Kim Bartley. "This is our most recent commitment to growth of our role in the community—emphasizing the importance of environmental concerns."

Even as it continues to satisfy those late-night burger cravings, White Castle is sharing its success with the community, giving more than $1.5 million annually to charitable organizations. In 2010-2011, White Castle raised more than $1 million for Autism Speaks, including funds from sales of a White Castle hamburger-scented candle.

For more information, visit www.whitecastle.com.

PHOTO CREDITS

Unless otherwise indicated, all images are listed left to right.

Page ii: © Walter Bibikow / age fotostock. Page v: © David Coleman / Alamy. Page vi: © Brad Feinknopf. Page x: © Walter Bibikow / age fotostock. Page xii, 1: © Natalie Boyne. Page xii, left: © Randall L. Schieber. Page 1, right: © Stan Rohrer / Alamy. Page 2, left: © Matthew Kazmierski. Page 2, 3: © © DGOlshavsky. Page 3, right: © SG cityscapes / Alamy. Page 4, left: © Greg Ashman/Corbis. Page 4, 5: © Brad Davis. Page 5, right: © Scott Stuart/ZUMA Press/Corbis. Page 6: Courtesy Library of Congress. Page 7, left: © Brad Feinknopf. Page 7, right: © Green Stock Media / Alamy. Page 8: © Amy Youngs. Page 9: © SG cityscapes / Alamy. Page 10: © Brad Feinknopf. Page 12: © Randall L. Schieber. Page 13: © rtyree1. Page 14, left: © Brad Feinknopf. Page 14, right: © Stan Rohrer / Alamy. Page 15: © Brad Feinknopf. Page 16: Courtesy Greater Columbus Convention & Visitors Bureau.Photo by Randall L. Schieber. Page 17, left: © Brad Feinknopf. Page 17, right: © Tim Perdue. Page 18, left: © SG cityscapes / Alamy. Page 18, right: © Randall L. Schieber. Page 19: © David Savage. Page 20: © Brad Feinknopf. Page 21, left: © Brad Feinknopf. Page 21, right: © Adam Schweigert. Page 22: © Brad Feinknopf. Page 23: © Antonin Borgeaud / Interlinks Image. Page 24: © Brad Feinknopf. Page 25: © Aaron Josefczyk/Icon SMI/Corbis. Page 26: Courtesy Columbus State Community College. Photo by Paul Rehg. Page 27, left: Courtesy Ohio Wesleyan University. Page 27, right: Courtesy Otterbein University. Page 28: Courtesy Ohio Supercomputer Center (OSC). Page 29: Courtesy Lincoln Street Studio. © Steven Elbert. Page 30: © Blend_Images. Page 31: © SG cityscapes / Alamy. Page 32, left: Courtesy The Ohio State University. Page 32, right: © airportrait. Page 33: © Rick Buchanan Photography. Page 34: © Wavebreak Media Ltd. Page 35, left: © mediaphotos. Page 35, right: Courtesy Nationwide Children's Hospital. Photo by Dan Smith. Page 36: Courtesy Cardinal Health. Page 37: Courtsey Medco Health Solutions, Inc. Page 38: Courtesy ABB. Photo by Halvor Molland. Page 39: © SG cityscapes / Alamy. Page 40, left: Courtesy Worthington Industries. Page 40, right: © Ringo Chiu/ZUMA Press/Corbis. Page 41: © Zhang Jun/Xinhua Press/Corbis. Page 42: Courtesy Limited Brands. Page 43: © Bill Bachmann / Alamy. Page 44: © Brad Feinknopf. Page 45: © Image Source Limited / Index Stock Imagery. Page 46: Courtesy Norfolk Southern. Page 47: © blueone. Page 48: © JT Hearn. Page 49, left: Courtesy Columbus Regional Airport Authority. Page 49, right: © Joe Sohm / Visions of America, LLC / Alamy. Page 50: Courtesy Moody-Nolan. Photo by Michael Houghton/STUDIOHIO. Page 51, left: © Gary Brown. Page 51, right: © SV Luma. Page 52: © JJRD. Page 53, left: © geckolo. Page 53, right: © ccat82. Page 54: © Troels Graugaard. Page 56: © José Luis Gutiérrez. Page 61: © Nikada. Page 62: © Tim Pohl. Page 66: © Jacob Wackerhausen. Page 76: © Joshua Hodge Photography. Page 87: Courtesy Otterbein University. Page 88: © Alex Slobodkin. Page 93: © Imagehit International Ltd. Page 94: © Masterfile (Royalty-Free Div.). Page 102: © Masterfile (Royalty-Free Div.). Page 108: © kali9. Page 120: © Rudyanto Wijaya. Page 126: © nyul. Page 137: © LdF. Page 138: © Image Source/Corbis.

cherbo publishing group, inc.

TYPOGRAPHY

Principal faces used: Univers, designed by Adrian Frutiger in 1957;

Helvetica, designed by Matthew Carter, Edouard Hoffmann,

and Max Miedinger in 1959

HARDWARE

Macintosh MacPro towers, digital color laser printing with Xerox Phaser 7400

SOFTWARE

QuarkXPress, Adobe CS5.5 Suite, Adobe Acrobat Pro, Microsoft Word, Eye-One Match by X-Rite, FlightCheck by Markzware

PAPER

Text Paper: #80 Luna Matte

Bound in Rainbow® recycled content papers from Ecological Fibers, Inc.

Dust Jacket: #100 Sterling-Litho Gloss